and the ~~heat~~ nibbles of
glint in the to & fro

his face jams
to the wrenched ~~the~~
blind ~~this~~ this way that ~~this path~~ so
nor ~~it~~ no ventaile to the ~~eus the~~
clampt ~~down~~ but dark un ~~tree~~ morning

then stretch. still where weeds hatten
the ~~chalk~~ predella.

& by Quilt takes over
~~still~~ unkindly
to the
wrenched over trit-trot
blind fingering
ventaile. to the
across the morning
quite
then stretch ∧ still where weeds
chalk predella.
and ~~by~~ T. Quilt takes over.

DAVID JONES

David Jones (1895–1974) was born and brought up in Brockley, then in Kent, south-east of London. At fourteen, he began studying at the Camberwell School of Arts and Crafts. During the Great War, he served for four years as a private, mostly with the London Welsh battalion of the Royal Welch Fusiliers. After the war, he resumed studying art, entered the Catholic Church in 1921, and became a close friend of the sculptor Eric Gill. In 1928 he began exhibiting with the Seven and Five Society in London. He was one of the foremost engravers and painters in England when in 1928 he began writing his first poem, *In Parenthesis* (1937), an epic based on his experience in the trenches. Its completion was delayed by a nervous breakdown in 1932 caused partly by his experiences in combat. After a second breakdown in 1948, he wrote *The Anathemata* (1952), a multi-voiced, epic-length, symbolic anatomy of western culture. *Epoch and Artist* (1959), a collection of his essays on art and culture that make explicit the original theory of culture informing his poetry. In his later years, suffering from depression and living and working in a series of rented rooms in London and Harrow, he painted important works, whose subjects include figures from myth and legend and flowers in glass chalices, and he painted lettered inscriptions. He was poor but beloved of many friends and received a steady stream of visitors. At the end of his life he published *The Sleeping Lord* (1974), containing his most accessible, mid-length poems.

THE AUTHOR

Thomas Dilworth is a Professor in the English Department at the University of Windsor, Ontario; a Killam Fellow; and a Fellow of the Royal Society of Canada. He has published widely on Modern literature and Romantic poetry and is the author of *Reading David Jones* (2008) and *The Shape of Meaning in the Poetry of David Jones* (1988), which won the British Council Prize in the Humanities. He edited Jones's illustrated *Rime of the Ancient Mariner* (2005), Jones's *Wedding Poems* (2002), and *Inner Necessities: the Letters of David Jones to Desmond Chute* (1984). He is publishing critical introductions and afterwords for bilingual (English/French) editions of *The Anathemata, The Sleeping Lord* and *The Ancient Mariner* and is currently writing Jones's biography. He co-edited *The Letters of Gertrude Stein and Virgil Thomson: Composition as Conversation* (2009). His recent poetry has appeared in *The Common Sky, Notre Dame Review, Rampike, Salmagundi, Ontario Review, Poetry* (Chicago), and *Windsor Review*.

THOMAS DILWORTH

DAVID JONES
IN THE GREAT WAR

with illustrations by David Jones

ENITHARMON PRESS

First published in 2012
by Enitharmon Press
26B Caversham Road
London NW5 2DU

www.enitharmon.co.uk

Distributed in the UK by
Central Books
99 Wallis Road
London E9 5LN

Distributed in the USA and Canada
by Dufour Editions Inc.
PO Box 7, Chester Springs
PA 19425, USA

ISBN: 978-1-907587-24-5

Enitharmon Press gratefully acknowledges a publishing grant
for this title from the Welsh Books Council,
and the financial support of Arts Council England
through Grants for the Arts.

British Library Cataloguing-in-Publication Data.
A catalogue record for this book is available
from the British Library.

Designed in Albertina by Libanus Press
and printed in England by
Antony Rowe Ltd

Frontispiece: David Jones in 1915

In memory of Thomas Murphy Dilworth, expelled from the US Naval Air Force for barnstorming by Admiral Chester Nimitz, who suppressed his records so that he could re-enlist as a pilot in the Eighth Air Force, in which he flew B-24 bombers and, against long odds, survived thirty missions and three crash landings to help raise seven children and die in bed in his ninety-third year.

For his granddaughters Alison, Molly and Christine and great-grandson Zachary, for his youngest son, Mike, who loves military history, and

for William Blissett, who in 1969 in his fourth-year seminar on the literature of the Great War devoted an entire semester to *In Parenthesis*.

CONTENTS

LIST OF ILLUSTRATIONS

Ownership of the images listed below is designated as follows: IWM (Imperial War Museum), NLW (National Library of Wales), NMW (National Museum of Wales), RWF (Regimental Museum of the Royal Welch Fusiliers), and T (Trustees of the Estate of David Jones). Copyright for all David Jones's visual art belongs to the Trustees.

ACKNOWLEDGEMENTS

The trustees of David Jones's estate gave generous permission to publish Jones's pictures and selections from his unpublished manuscripts. William Blissett introduced me to Jones's writing and then to the writer. Jones's close friends Tom Burns, Harman Grisewood and Stanley Honeyman, and his oldest friends, Philip Hagreen, Jim Ede and Petra Tegetmeier, were my most important living sources. Others who shared memories or gave access to letters are Julian Asquith, Sarah and Maurice Balme, David Blamires, William Blissett, Morag Bulbrook, Solange Dayras, Bee Dufort, Mollie Elkin, Arthur Giardelli, Nicolete Gray, René and Joan Hague, Ernest Hawkins, Paul Hills, Edward Hodgkin, Colin Hughes, Tony Hyne, Kathleen Lockitt, John Montague, Peter Orr, David Poulter, Nancy Sandars, Richard Shirley-Smith, Elizabeth and Christopher Skelton, Janet Stone, Tony Stoneburner, Colin Wilcockson, Juliet Wood, Stella Wright and Valerie Wynne-Williams. Tony Stoneburner gave me access to notes on conversations with Jones. Honeyman and Michael Snapes answered military questions. To Honeyman especially but also to others listed here and to their spouses I am indebted for kindness, hospitality, and encouragement – as I am also to the poet and editor Robin Robertson, who read much of this book and suggested improvements. So did Wilcockson and Blissett. Stephen Stuart-Smith, Peter Target and Tom Durham helped with final corrections, and Stuart-Smith, with the typographer Michael Mitchell, saw to the printing of text and pictures with the care and high standards typical of Enitharmon Press.

I received information or photographs from Jones's trustees and Peter Chasseaud, Derek Shiel and John Skelton. Nicholas Elkin supplied photographs of drawings. Huw Ceiriog Jones helped in many ways, as did Daniel Huws and Philip Davies in the late 1980s at the National Library of Wales. In its collection are most of Jones's manuscripts, papers and books. The letters to Jim Ede are at Kettle's Yard in Cambridge, those to Harman Grisewood at the Beinecke Library at Yale, those to René Hague at the University of Toronto Fisher Rare Book Library, those to Kenneth Clark, Peter Levi and Janet Stone at the Bodleian in Oxford, and those to Helen Sutherland are in the Tate Gallery Archive. Audio recordings of my interviews are in the Kelly Library, St Michael's College, University of Toronto. The most important published biographical sources are *Dai Greatcoat*, edited by Hague (1980), and Blissett's *The Long Conversation* (1981). Colin Hughes's *The Man Who Was on the Field:* In Parenthesis *as Straight Reporting* (1979) recounts the experience of Jones in his battalion during the months culminating in the Battle of the Somme. While indebted to these works, I chiefly use unpublished sources, mainly letters, battalion diaries and tape-recorded interviews.

The Social Science and Humanities Research Council of Canada generously funded my research. So did a Killam Fellowship and a University of Windsor Humanities Research Fellowship.

ABBREVIATIONS FOR WORKS BY DAVID JONES

A   *The Anathemata.* London: Faber and Faber, 1972.

IP   *In Parenthesis.* London: Faber and Faber, 1978.

DGC   *Dai Greatcoat*, ed. René Hague. London: Faber and Faber, 1980.

SL   *The Sleeping Lord.* London: Faber and Faber, 1974.

WP   *Wedding Poems*, ed. Thomas Dilworth. London: Enitharmon Press, 2002.

INTRODUCTION

David Jones is one of the great modernists. He was already an important engraver and painter when he wrote his epic poem of the Great War, *In Parenthesis* (1937), which is one of the foremost works of British literary Modernism.* Jones's second epic-length poem, *The Anathemata* (1952), is a symbolic, dramatic anatomy of western culture – a work which Eliot thought established him as a writer 'of major importance', placing him in the company of himself (Eliot), James Joyce and Ezra Pound.¹ Jones subsequently published *The Sleeping Lord* (1974), containing mostly mid-length poems, which Seamus Heaney said enriches 'not only the language but people's consciousness of who they have been and who they consequently are'.² If, as Jones himself seems to have thought, he was a better poet than visual artist, he was nevertheless an important visual artist, and among his engravings, his pictures of legendary and mythic figures, his still-lifes, and his painted inscriptions (a form he invented) are masterpieces. Many are in galleries in Britain (most in the National Museum of Wales and the Tate Gallery) and elsewhere throughout the world. Kenneth Clark thought him the best modern British painter.³ Jones also wrote several important essays formulating an original and convincing theory of culture, which, according to the New York art critic Harold Rosenberg, is 'the axiomatic precondition for understanding contemporary creation'.⁴

Among the important modernists, David Jones was one of the

---

* That *In Parenthesis* is an epic is not in doubt: most initial reviewers, following T. S. Eliot (writing the blurb for its first publication), announced it as such. Whether it is a poem, however, has been questioned since it is only partially verse; but verse and poetry are not synonymous – they differ categorically. Verse is merely writing in end-lines instead of run-on lines, whereas poetry is language used to its maximum potential. Because of its richness, the language of *In Parenthesis* is poetry, whether verse or not.

few who served in that horrendous epiphany of modernity, the Great War.

As a young man, he saw more active service than any other British war writer – a claim that has been made for Edmund Blunden, but mistakenly. Jones served in the army seven months longer than Blunden. Even with time subtracted for convalescence and leave, he spent a total of 117 weeks at the front, which is at least two months longer than Blunden, half a year longer than Isaac Rosenberg, twice as long as Siegfried Sassoon and Ivor Gurney, and more than twice as long as Wilfred Owen, Charles Sorley, Robert Graves, and Wyndham Lewis. Like Rosenberg and Gurney, Jones was a private, so his experience was more onerous, though less dangerous, than that of most other war writers, who were junior officers. His military service was extensive and powerfully influenced much of his subsequent creative work.

This book would be considerably longer if the hinge-word in its title were 'and' instead of 'in'. 'David Jones and the Great War' would include the writing and publication of *In Parenthesis*, which is based on his first seven months in the trenches, culminating in the assault on Mametz Wood during the Battle of the Somme. It would also include his correction of the historical record for the second Christmas in the trenches – made on page 216 of *The Anathemata*. It would include his wedding poem 'Prothalamion', which makes reference to his experience at Passchendaele (*WP* 32-3); and it would include all the mid-length poems in *The Sleeping Lord*, which are informed by his military experience, especially the final poem, 'The Book of Balaam's Ass', whose subject is a suicidal assault by his battalion at Passchendaele.

His war experience was often harrowing. In this book I hope to dispel forever the assumption that he simply enjoyed the war and suffered no negative consequences from it. That notion originated with his close friend René Hague, who was highly intelligent, a gifted linguist, but psychologically naïve and knew Jones only since December 1924. It is true that Jones never complained about his experiences in the trenches and was often amusing about them. But Frank

Medworth and Harold Weaver Hawkins were his two closest art-school friends, they both served (and were wounded) on the Western Front, and they knew him well both before and immediately after the war; and it was their opinion that Jones suffered from shell shock. He subsequently suffered two severe nervous breakdowns owing largely to what we now call post-traumatic stress disorder. Psychological factors contributed to these breakdowns, and I will discuss them in his full biography, but had he not served in the trenches, he would never have suffered emotionally as he did. His first breakdown, in 1932, initiated four decades of depression, which he was only partly able to counteract by creative work.

The result of that work is impressive. It includes what are arguably the two greatest long poems of the twentieth century, other poetry of an equally high calibre, and many wonderful paintings and painted inscriptions. That he finished all this work while suffering his own dark interior aftermath of the war establishes him, I think, as a hero of creative imagination. His experience of combat haunted him. He habitually told war anecdotes to visitors, of whom, in the last years of his life, I was one. (By consulting battalion diaries, I have been able to date precisely some of the personal experiences he related.) A book entitled *David Jones and the Great War* would have somehow to encompass all of the fifty-six years of his postwar life.

Instead of 'and', however, the hinge-word in the title is 'in', and so, apart from Chapters 1 and 9, I focus on his experiences during the war – experiences that underlie *In Parenthesis* but go far beyond the compass of its narrative. A slice of biography, the present book depicts Jones as he then was, naïvely idealistic and romantic; not the mature artist and poet he would become, sceptical about all things political and immune to jingoism. While this is his war story, it also involves the histories of the units he served with: the 15th Battalion (London Welsh) of the Royal Welch Fusiliers (23rd Foot); the 2nd Field Survey Company, at Second Army Headquarters; and the 3rd Battalion Royal Welch Fusiliers stationed at Limerick, Ireland. His military experience was varied as well as long.

I reproduce many of his war sketches and, for the first time since the war, eight fully rendered drawings. The sketches are of infantry-men, landscapes, ruined villages, and still-lifes – all works of documentary realism, all done in pencil. Some of them are fully achieved portraits but most done in the trenches are quickly rendered and cartoonish.* Showing them in 1960 to his friend and fellow ex-service-man the Welsh nationalist and writer Saunders Lewis, Jones called them 'bloody awful aesthetically' but of 'sentimental interest for blokes like ourselves who saw it all'.⁵ Unlike these sketches, the eight finished drawings were meant for public viewing – five of them photographically reproduced in *The Graphic* during the war; the others self-published (with the help of his father, who was a printer's overseer) as covers of two greetings cards and an allegorical pamphlet. Unlike the simpler sketches, all but two of these eight drawings visually associate the present with the distant past and convey political allegiance and moral judgment. They express the values of most of the contemporary civilian population, which Private Jones evidently shared – views which, in the years following the war, he came to see as ludicrously naïve. Ashamed of the idealism and chauvinism of his published drawings, he burnt the originals in 1926 along with most of his earlier work, which he no longer liked. Only the published versions survive. About these pictures he kept mum. Since their publication, they have not been attributed to him till now.

Published here for the first time are photographs of Jones, his friends, and the girl he first fell in love with as an adult. Here also are Jones's three earliest writings for a public readership, published in full for the first time: 'A French Vision' (19 October 1916), 'A Soldier's Letter Home' (17 May 1917) and *The Quest* (November 1917).

Because so much of his visual art is reproduced here, I describe in the first chapter the training Jones received as an art student before the war. In this chapter I also indicate the breadth of his reading during

---

* All but seven of these 'war sketches' are reproduced by Anthony Hyne in *David Jones, A Fusilier at the Front* (Bridgend: Seren, 1995). Those appearing here for the first time are: figs. 9, 11, 14, 15, 34, 60 and 65.

childhood and adolescence in order to convey the interests, the level of intelligence and the bent of imagination of the young man who went to war. Together with his Christian faith, these conditioned his response to the worst of all wars for infantrymen and largely allowed him subsequently to interpret it in what is probably the greatest literary work on war in English.

Information from my four visits to Jones – shared with William Blissett, who records them in *The Long Conversation* (1981) – comes, unless otherwise specified, from my memory of them. To economise on endnotes, in the chapters that follow I group citations in a single note at the end of each paragraph or series of related paragraphs, listing citations in order of reference but eliminating repeat-citations within a note. I conducted all interviews cited that are not attributed by name to another interviewer. Whenever I cite a letter from Jones, I indicate only the person to whom he writes and the date. When not in a footnote, the citation for that note is included in the endnote to the paragraph to which the footnote belongs.

I was in my mid-twenties when I visited David Jones in 1971 and 1972. He was then in his mid-seventies and living in Calvary Nursing Home in Harrow. He spoke from a great depth of mind, often with strong feeling, in a richly timbred voice, deliberately and with hesitation. He seemed to me a man of genius, but I was most struck by his being more warmly affectionate than any other man I had met. This sense of him was shared by his many friends and acquaintances, most of whom I came to know in the course of researching his full biography, to which this book is a prelude and of which its war chapters are an expansion. That remarkable personal warmth must have characterised the nineteen-year-old who went off to war in 1915.

NOTES

1   'A Note of Introduction', *In Parenthesis* (London: Faber, 1961), p. viii.
2   *The Spectator* (4 May 1974), p. 547.
3   Janet Stone, close friend of Clark, interviewed 2 October 1987.
4   *The New Yorker*, 22 August 1964, p. 122. For a brief account of Jones's cultural theory, see Thomas Dilworth, *Reading David Jones* (Cardiff: University of Wales, 2008), pp. 3–4.
5   To Saunders Lewis, 6 July 1960.

CHAPTER 1

PRE-WAR (1895–1914)

David Jones, the boy who went to war, was in many ways typical of his generation. A product of the late-Victorian, early Edwardian lower-middle class, he was imbued with idealistic, patriotic, imperialist values. But in his devotion to drawing and his breadth of reading, he was exceptional.

Jones was born on 1 November 1895, the third child of a lower-middle-class family in Brockley, soon to become a suburb of London. His mother was a Thames-side Londoner, who, before marrying, had been a governess, a Sunday-school teacher, and a gifted amateur draftswoman. His father was a native North Welshman who worked as a printer's overseer for The Christian Herald Company. They were both Church of England. She was inclined to be High Church but deferred to the evangelicalism of her husband, who was a lay preacher. Their third child was christened Walter David Jones but from an early age felt affinity with his father's native Wales and disliked his Anglo-Saxon first name, so that by the age of 'eight or nine' he managed to have family and friends call him David.[1] Both parents encouraged him to draw and paint, and, before the age of ten he was producing vivid, intensely felt animal drawings and paintings and showing them publicly in national children's exhibitions. His father regularly brought home a great many newspapers and magazines, and from about the age of thirteen David imitated the style of illustrations in them.

He was exposed early to the written word. At church and at home, before he could read, he heard the language of the Authorised Version of the Bible and the Book of Common Prayer. In addition, his parents subscribed to the Books for the Bairns' series of monthly literary volumes. David wanted read to him 'always Arthurian things', and his favourite in the series was *King Arthur and the Knights of the Round Table* (1899), an adaptation of stories from *The Mabinogion* and Sir Thomas Malory. To him the most impressive was 'Prince Geraint and Fair Enid', in which Geraint avenges an insult to Guinevere by defeating the Knight of the Sparrow Hawk, a bully and a thief. His mother read these stories to him, and he paid his older sister a penny an hour to read them aloud.[2] Like them, many of the stories and books he subsequently read were romances. The types in them – good knight, bad knight, damsel – would inform his finished war drawings.

While attending Brockley Road School, he read Roman and British history. He was impressed by Cloelia, a Roman girl who escaped the Etruscans by swimming the Tiber (which he thought was as wide as the Thames at London Bridge). He learned about the Roman conquest of Britain and was made to memorise Cowper's poem about Boadicea, the 'British warrior-queen / Bleeding from the Roman rods'.[3] He already knew about her from the May 1901 volume in the Books for Bairns series, which opens to a frontispiece depicting 'Boadicea, Queen of the Iceni, calling upon the Britons to defend their country against the Romans'.* He was aware of the wars in France – in 1905 he painted a small watercolour of *Edward III Entering Calais, 1347*.

The history he and the others of his generation learned at school was chauvinistic. He was taught, for example, that the English fought the Hundred Years War against 'the tyrant's yoke' (see ch. 5, p. 128) and won it on the strength of the victories at Crécy and Agincourt, but he was not told about the subsequent French reconquest. Pervading his reading was Victorian admiration of the Romans as precursors to the English in spreading enlightened civilization.[4] He read the patriotic stories in the Union Jack Library. On Empire Day, he and his schoolmates sang Kipling's 'Recessional', whose theme is that

---

* He tended to remain loyal to youthful enthusiasms. When in 1961 *The Times* published an article praising Boadicea for giving 'the Anglo-Saxons something to boast about at an extremely thin time in their history', he sent a letter (unpublished) asking what 'this Celtic queen' had to do with Anglo-Saxons and hoping that, in Belloc's words, 'the truth might be allowed to prevail a bit.'

imperialism is ethical if imperialists are humble and contrite.

Later, in a manuscript draft of *In Parenthesis,* he listed verbal expressions and topics indicative of the school culture of anyone of his generation:

> Below the belt. / Natives. / Sportsman. / Whiteman. / Boxing. / Sarawak. / Lower-deck. / Exports. / Club. / English woman-hood. / Port of London Authority. / Wide open spaces. / Dr. Livingstone. / Law of Gravitation. / North West Passage. / 'but not the six hundred'. / Stock Exchange. / Slave Trade. / Good wholesome food. / . . . sun never sets. / Royal Horse Show. / Royal Humane Society. / Royal Naval & Military Tournament. / Clean living. / Cricket. / Small Nations. / Gordon. / Kitchener. / Roberts. / Florence Nightingale. / Grace Darling. / Somehow, Dr. Nansen. / Nelson, who existed uncreated and who stood as he were Zeus, behind the Gods.

By the age of eight, Jones was devoted to Nelson and walked the two-and-a-half miles from Brockley across Blackheath to Greenwich Park to see the admiral's relics. On display in the upper Painted Hall of the Royal Naval College, where, almost a century earlier, Nelson's body had lain in state, were the objects the great man had handled, the uniform in which he died – the hole from the fatal musket ball visible below the left epaulette – and his blood-stained stockings. Jones walked there from Brockley several times, his interest most intense when he was nine, during the centenary celebration of the victory at Trafalgar. As a young boy, he 'was torn' in his hero-worshipping between English Nelson and Welsh Owen Glendower.[5] He felt himself to be Welsh, but his upbringing and native culture were English.

The manuscript list of significant expressions continues: 'Selfridge. / Lucknow. / Ladysmith. / St Lawrence. / Goodwin Sands. / Trinity House. / Beef Eater. / Tilbury. / Virgin Queen. / Open Bible. / Constitution. / Fine body of men.' About all these, he wrote that they 'aroused … directly, or by association an identical emotion, an attitude of adoration which we properly tender to that which makes and sustains us.'

Occasionally a naval commander would address the student body on 'the Bull-dog breed' and 'the Union Flag in very hot, and very cold places' and 'how the sea was free'. A history lesson in the fourth standard stressed 'the Inquisition and the habitual cruelty of foreign nations'. In England, 'Philanthropists and Policemen seemed to strive with each other in a race of which the goal and crown was a universal affability and kindness' (*IP* MS). For the children of the middle class at least, this was a nation of polite idealism, of public and private virtue sustained by convention and widespread, sincere Protestant Christianity. Except for the Court, Edwardian England remained culturally Victorian.

More than most of his generation and class, his personal reading took him deep into the national romance of imperial Britain, enriching it with historical and literary detail. In 1910, while his elder brother was dying of tuberculosis, David stayed in Brighton with his wealthy great-uncle Tom Pethybridge, a Gladstonian Liberal who celebrated the Glorious Revolution of 1688 and obliged him to read books.* Among these was J. R. Green's *Shorter History of the English People*, which Jones disliked for its Victorian Germanicist adulation of Anglo-Saxons at the expense of Celtic Britons. He read William Stubbs on constitutional law, J. A. Froude on Julius Caesar, Lord Macaulay's essays, and, most importantly, Macaulay's *Lays of Ancient Rome*. He memorised parts of 'Horatius' – he had to recite passages from memory for his great-uncle. Jones's favourite was 'The Battle of Lake Regillus'. Macaulay's verse was 'doggerel', he later said, 'but it got to me' and left 'an indelible mark – one never gets rid of these Roman

---

* The Pethybridge house in Brighton was not 'a converted old fortress or gun emplacement right on the shore' where 'spray would hit the windows' (Jonathan Miles and Derek Shiel, *David Jones, the Maker Unmade*, [Bridgend: Seren, 1995] p. 120), a mistake originating in William Blissett confusing the house with the Fort Hotel at Sidmouth, where Jones stayed in the 1930s and possibly with a house in Hove where his parents used to stay (*The Long Conversation*, p. 102).

things.' He had many long conversations with his great-uncle, who, the following year, sent him for his birthday Sebastian Evans's translation of Geoffrey of Monmouth (1904), inscribed to 'Walter David Jones, Champion of the Ancient Welsh from a converted Saxon' and, for his birthday in 1912, Lutzow's *Medieval Towns* (1907) inscribed to 'W.D.J. an introduction to a wider circle of knowledge.' Jones would later say of his great-uncle Tom, 'I owe him . . . quite a lot'.[6]

In 1910, at a Christmas celebration for his extended family, David Jones recited 'selections from *Henry V*' and 'Griffith's Answer to Harold', the refusal in 1063 of the Welsh king to surrender to Anglo-Saxon Harold Godwinson.[7] His selection indicates his continuing inner division between being English and identifying with the Welsh.

His adolescence was enriched with an abundance of inexpensive books. He went to Denny's Bookshop in the Strand to buy the shilling volumes published by Everyman Library and those published by the Home University Library and Temple Classics. He read and liked the early novels of H. G. Wells. He probably read J. G. Edgar's *Heroes of England* (1910) – decades later he would give a copy to his seven-year-old nephew. In 1956, he would read C. S. Lewis's autobiography and be '*astounded*' at their '*virtually identical*' reading as children and adolescents, except for things Welsh.[8] He therefore probably, like Lewis, read fiction about the ancient world: *Quo Vadis, Darkness and Dawn, The Gladiator, Ben Hur*. We know that he read Kipling's *Puck of Pook's Hill* and *Rewards and Fairies*, Lewis Carroll's Alice books, and 'a certain amount of English poetry', a favourite being *The Rime of the Ancient Mariner*. He also read pure romance. In 1910 he bought and began reading, 'in bits', the Everyman Library two-volume Malory. That year he was also reading Maurice Hewlett's modern romances of medieval intrigue, which borrow heavily from Malory and are spiced with bizarre eroticism. In 1913 he read Eugene Mason's translation of *Aucassin and Nicolette* (Dent, 1910), an authentic medieval romance about a knight in love with a lady which, without ever rereading, he would be able vividly to recall half a century later. Interest stirred by romance led to amateur scholarship. He bought and read H. J. Chaytor's *The Troubadours* (1912).

He read James Fenimore Cooper's *The Last of the Mohicans*. It sparked his 'first conscious awareness of a dichotomy' between civilization and 'indigenous cultures'. Sympathy with such cultures falling before powerful civilizations helps to account for his being unable 'to swallow' what he would call 'the nonsense about "progress" with a capital P'.[9] He saw similarity between the American Indian and the medieval Welsh.

1. Camberwell School of Arts and Crafts, 1910

At the age of fourteen, he left Brockley Road School for the Camberwell School of Arts and Crafts (fig. 1), where he continued his reading. The art school had only one required academic course, English Literature, which met for an hour one afternoon a week. For this course he read the Romantic poets, Matthew Arnold, novels by Scott, Thackeray, Austen and Dickens, and essays on art from Mandeville to Ruskin. It was probably for this class that he read Reynolds' *Discourses* and Emerson, whom he liked 'a good bit'. At this time, he read Ruskin avidly and considered him brilliant.[10]

As an adolescent he read, on his own or for class, translations of Bede and Gildas, *The Anglo-Saxon Chronicle*, the Norse sagas, and *The Song of Roland*. He read 'a little Chaucer'; William Langland; Shakespeare, 'mainly the historical plays' (he disliked most of the comedies) and *Macbeth*; John Skelton; Hugh Latimer's sermons; the Scottish ballads; 'some Milton'; Gibbon; 'bits of Coleridge'; Percy's *Reliques*; Browning; and the poetry of Rossetti and William Morris, who were then special 'enthusiasms'. He also read 'mythology, & things about the sea' and George Borrow, preferring *Lavengro* and *Romany Rye* to *Wild Wales*. He read Stowe's *Survey* of Elizabethan London.[11]

A large part of his reading concerned Wales. For birthdays his father bought him books on Welsh history and, hoping he would learn the language, Welsh grammar. Sometime before 1915, he read Owen M. Edwards' *Wales* and John Lloyd's great two-volume *The History of Wales from Early Times to 1282* (1911). This book he would always value as the best history of Wales in English. As the son of a North Welshman, he was interested to learn that the lineage of northern princely families was by far the most important to medieval Wales.[12] His father gave him for his sixteenth birthday *A Pocket Dictionary of Welsh–English* and John Rhys and David Brynmor-Jones's *The Welsh People* – the latter a broad grounding in Welsh history that would remain important to him. At nearly 700 pages, it is a full account of the Welsh from pre-Roman, continental beginnings to 1900. In addition to history, he read the Welsh triplets, Charlotte Guest's translation of *The Mabinogion*, Giraldus Cambrensis's *Itinerary and Description of Wales*, and the copy of Geoffrey of Monmouth given him by his great-uncle Tom. In 1913 he read Evans's *In Quest of the Holy Grail* (1898).[13] In the year of its publication, he read Lewis Jones's *King Arthur in History and Legend* (1914).

Before enlisting in the army his sensibility was historical and literary and his imagination thoroughly romantic. He had already read most of the works by which he would interpret his war experiences in *In Parenthesis*. Reviewers and critics would later complain that its allusions to history, myth, and literature would have been impossible for a young infantryman during the war. But Jones was, by the time of enlistment, exceptionally well-read, and he later told friends that the associations in the poem actually were the sort that occurred during the war to him and to others among his friends in the trenches.

His principal interest at Camberwell Art School was, of course, visual art. He studied 'Book Illustration, Composition and Drawing from Life', a flexible programme allowing for the retaking of courses. Those he repeated included Reginald Savage's 'Drawing and Design for Book Illustration and Composition' and A. S. Hartrick's 'Drawing and Painting the Draped Figure'.[14] Savage and Hartrick were the teachers who influenced him most.

Reginald Savage was a man of the 1890s, a book illustrator and former associate of Charles Ricketts, Charles Shannon, and Sturge Moore. He taught the work of the great nineteenth-century illustrators: George Pinwell, Frederick Sandys, Aubrey Beardsley, and Louis Boutet de Monvel. For Savage, the history of art culminated in the Pre-Raphaelites. He was a romantic medievalist and had his students draw studies of figures in medieval costume.[15]

Jones's choice of subject to draw was nearly always medieval, and

2. *David Jones as Robin Hood, and his friends Harold Weaver Hawkins and Frank Medworth*

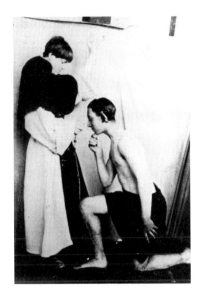

3. *David Jones as Friar*   4. *David Jones as Bard*

he was soon, like Savage, enamoured of the Pre-Raphaelites. With staged poses and settings implying narrative, his work reflects the Victorian story-telling impulse which pervaded Camberwell, where art was seen as an extension of writing, usually historical and often medieval in subject. There were courses in Costume Design and Dressmaking, in which female students produced historical clothing worn by models and by other students posing in tableaux, and performing skits. Students photographed in these costumes include Jones dressed as Robin Hood (fig. 2) – beside him, his closest art-student friends Harold Weaver Hawkins, dressed homonymously as a herald, and Frank Medworth, dressed as a knight. There are also photographs of Jones dressed as a friar blessing a half-naked barbarian (fig. 3) and as an eclectic bard with harp, Saxon cross-gartering and Viking helmet (fig. 4). Historical dress and interiors were part of the curriculum. Savage had them go on Saturdays to the Victoria and Albert Museum to sketch the period rooms. Jones and his friends probably went to the Tower of London to sketch the armour and weapons – he had gone there once with a schoolmate before enrolling in Camberwell.[16]

The most accomplished and best connected artist teaching in the school was A. S. Hartrick. He had known Whistler and Beardsley in London, and Degas, Gauguin and Toulouse-Lautrec in France, where he had been a close friend of Van Gogh. Hartrick noticed immediately that Jones was drawing badly and diagnosed the cause as imitation of the contemporary newspaper and magazine illustrations that his father had brought home from work. As a corrective, Hartrick urged direct observation of the subject. 'Trust what you see', he said, 'not what you know.' He stressed his own basic doctrine of sincerity as the chief artistic virtue – sincerity being for him the subordination of technique to perception integrated with feeling. Sincerity had been, he said, the source of originality in Gauguin, forcing him to go 'back to beginnings' and touch nature 'with emotion'.[17]

Hartrick had his students begin by looking at the model for some minutes before drawing. He told them: mentally observe the chief characteristics that will govern your treatment from start to finish. See relationships. Then lightly draw the general outline. He had learned at the Académie Julian the conventional practice of working paper with chalk, charcoal, and India-rubber as a prelude to painting but he had rejected that. See and draw first the silhouette of an object. Forget for the moment mass and tone. Contour is the beginning of all the best drawing. 'Look at the outline', he said, 'and you will see the form, which is the object of drawing.'[18]

He taught Jones how to draw in two styles. The first was by using a thick, emphatic contour line that merges into shading. The Pre-Raphaelites and Millet drew this way, as did Degas. They belong, he said, to a tradition of drawing that extends back through Poussin and Rubens to Michelangelo. Jones adopted this style, visible in his picture of a soldier being advised by an old man (fig. 5), signed 'W. David Jones, 1914'. It would be the style of his drawings until the late 1920s, including the finished drawings he would make during the war. In this 1914 drawing, the soldier's prominent chin is an idealised version of Jones's chin – like many young artists, he drew faces resembling his own, as he would also in his finished war drawings.

The other style – drawing the contour thinly, with the point – would be that of his informal war sketches and his drawings and paintings after 1927. Hartrick was convinced that this style makes the best draughtsmen. Stressing it in his teaching above the other style, he said he had learned it at the Slade from Legros, who had learned it from his teacher Ingres, who had discovered it in Raphael and the earlier Italian masters. Drawing with the point had the advantage, he said, of eliminating subjective self-expression and personal mannerisms. Exemplars of this style included Degas (sometimes) and the mid-century newspaper and magazine illustrators, who had drawn for facsimile-reproduction by wood engravers. Hartrick praised especially Frederick Walker and, pre-eminently, Charles Keene of *Punch*,

5. Soldier Advised by Old Man, *1914*

whom he called 'the most original of all British draughtsmen ... and in his way one of the great artists of the nineteenth century'. Savage, too, praised these illustrators.[19]

Hartrick urged drawing contour with the point as the essence of 'Classical' art. Everything else, including the more thickly drawn line, was, he said, 'Romantic'. Outline is, he said, the classical basis against which the feeling, planes, detail, shadow and atmosphere establish art as romantic. The development of most of the great western painters, even those who began with the classical, was towards 'pure Romance', which justifies the breaking of classical rules. Drawing only really becomes art, he said, when it goes beyond precision of representation and communicates emotion. In 1939 Hartrick would declare his conviction that his former student David Jones was 'an incurable romantic'.[20]

He fired Jones's enthusiasm for drawing for its own sake and not merely as a prelude to painting. By this point Jones was drawing continually at Hartrick's urging, and he was now drawing well.

Hartrick would sometimes look at one of his pictures and say to the class, 'Look at that, you see, Jones leaves out everything but the magic', and Jones, though embarrassed, was delighted. 'It was', he remembered at the end of his life, 'the nicest thing ever said about my work.' But Hartrick did not always praise. When the work was too tentative or elaborate, he would say, 'Make a frank statement, Jones, make a frank statement.'[21]

Hartrick introduced him and the other students to the work of the best living journalistic and book illustrators, whom he knew personally. Since 1889, he had worked as a draughtsman for *The Graphic* and in the early 1890s drew for *The Daily Graphic*, the *Pall Mall Budget* and the *Pall Mall Magazine*. Hartrick was still associated with *The Graphic*, and would arrange for Jones to publish drawings there during the war.

Hartrick insisted on memory-drawing. He had students copy an old master's work, put the copy away, and later redraw it from memory. In the redrawing, they were to forget incidental details and retain the essentials of design. During such an exercise, Jones copied Rubens's *Judgment of Paris* in the National Gallery, which he later remembered as a 'bloody difficult' task.[22] Stressing the importance of memory-training for the imaginative painter, Hartrick talked of his friend the illustrator Phil May following a person whose appearance he wanted to capture through the streets of London for ten minutes and then being able to draw him or her accurately from memory from any angle with any facial expression.[23] Practice in memory-drawing would sometimes bear fruit in Jones's trench sketches.

He later said that he learned more from Hartrick than from any other teacher, and certainly no one who later taught or influenced him – not Walter Bayes, Walter Sickert or Eric Gill – would ever have as much impact on him as an artist. For Jones, 'Mr. Hartrick' (as he always called him) was an artistic father-figure and model of insight and sensitivity. He liked best about his teacher's best work that it was 'lyrical', 'tentative', and with a 'sense of design & understanding of form'.[24] These attributes would also be those of Jones's best work.

Jones's friend Medworth received his art teacher's certificates on 18 March 1913, and the occasion was, for a group of them, a sort of graduation. Photographs were taken. Jones joined in, posing indoors and on the front steps of the main entrance to the school (fig. 6). In one photograph, his hair plastered with oil and parted in the middle, he is the best-dressed in the group and the only one with a walking stick – evidently a bit of a dandy. It was the age of low-cut coats, of the 'knut', and of spread ties with pins. Later, despite poverty, he would always be fussy about what he wore, preferring the best quality in clothes and shoes – a sartorial inclination apparently well established before the war.[25] Just behind him is Medworth, and on the far left (the viewer's right), Hawkins.

Unlike Medworth, Jones refused to take the Board of Education national examinations to qualify as an art master. Like the Impressionists Hartrick praised, he was determined to dedicate himself entirely to 'fine art'. He also decided that his vocation precluded working as a commercial artist – Hartrick had hurt himself as an

6. David Jones and friends, 18 March 1913

artist, Jones thought, by working commercially, which diminishes autonomous development and relegates important work to something like a hobby. Jones wanted to draw animals and to illustrate historical subjects, preferably those of medieval Welsh history and legend, but he had no idea how to earn a living at it.[26] Pessimistic about his economic prospects, he decided while at Camberwell that his artistic vocation precluded supporting a wife and family, so, in principle (with no prospective bride on the horizon), he resolved to forgo marriage. Saying no to commercial art meant poverty. Without earning money, he would have to continue living with his parents and, while he remained in school, they would have to pay his fees.[27]

NOTES TO CHAPTER 1

1 To Valerie Wynne Williams, 5 April 1962, unposted.

2 DJ recorded by Arthur Giardelli, 1965; 'Sign of the bear, David Jones talks to Nesta Roberts', *Guardian*, 17 February 1964; 'Fragments of an Attempted Autobiographical Writing', p. 104.

3 Letter draft frag. n.d.; *DG* 186; to Kathleen Raine frag. n.d.; to René Hague, 29 February 1960; to *The Times*, 22 February 1961.

4 To Harman Grisewood, 15–24 April 1972.

5 To Saunders Lewis, 9 April 1970; to Harman Grisewood, 1 February 1971; to Arthur Giardelli, 9-11 August 1973; to Saunders Lewis, 9 April 1970; DJ in conversation with Tony Stoneburner, written record 26 May 1969; 7 June 1969; to Jackson Knight, 11 October 1952.

6 DJ in conversation with Tony Stoneburner, written record 9 June 1966; to Harman Grisewood, 9 October 1971; 13 March 1942; DJ in conversation with the author, 24 August 1972; to Harman Grisewood, 9 October 1971; DJ in conversation with Tony Stoneburner, written record 9 June 1966; to Tony Stoneburner, 5 August 1969.

7 Maurice Bradshaw to Stella Wright, 20 August 1976.

8 Letter intended for publication frag. n.d.; to Harman Grisewood, 1 September 1956.

9 To Tom Burns, 17 October 1971; to René Hague, December 1933; to Harman Grisewood, 7 May 1964; to Tony Stoneburner, 25 June 1967.

10 To Granny Ede, 27 September 1949; to Helen Sutherland, 17 October 1943; DJ to Philip Hagreen, interviewed 11 June 1991.

11 Letter draft frag. n.d.; to René Hague, 9-15 July 1973; to Tony Stoneburner, 30 August 1963; to René Hague, 22 December 1933; to John H. Johnston, 2 May 1962; to Helen Sutherland, 29 September 1958; to Tony Stoneburner, 30 August 1963.

12 DJ 'Some Notes on the Difficulties of one Writer of Welsh affinity whose language is English', typescript for Vernon Watkins, 11 April 1962; printed in *DG*; to Vernon Watkins, 5 April 1962; to Mr Emlyn-Davies, 19 June 1964; DJ in conversation with Tony Stoneburner, written record 26 May 1969.

13 Letter draft frag. n.d.; to Harman Grisewood, 18 May 1956; to Aneirin Talfan Davies, 17-18 February 1959; to Meic Stephens, 27 February 1973; to René Hague, 27 September 1963, 11 August 1974; to Saunders Lewis, 14 June 1972.

14 To Nicolete Gray, 4 April 1961; Ernest Hawkins, interviewed 15 June 1988.

15 Robin Ironside, *David Jones* (Harmondsworth, Middlesex: Penguin, 1949), p. 5; to Jim Ede, 15 April 1943.

16 To René Hague, 12 April 1936; Edward Hodgkin, interviewed 1 August 1987, 1 September 1987; Howard Grimmet to DJ, 10 January 1955.

17 A. S. Hartrick, *Drawing* (London: Pitman, 1921), pp. 54–7.

18 A. S. Hartrick, *Drawing*, pp. 54–7; *A Painter's Pilgrimage Through Fifty Years* (Cambridge: Cambridge University Press, 1939), pp. 8, 37.

19 Hartrick, *A Painter's Pilgrimage*, p. 95; DJ in conversation with author, 24 August 1972.

20 Hartrick, *Drawing*, pp. 38–41, 5; *A Painter's Pilgrimage*, pp. 233–4.

21 DJ to William Blissett, *The Long Conversation* (Oxford: Oxford University Press, 1981), p. 44; Sarah Balme interviewed 17 June 1990; to Valerie Wynne Williams, 12 May 1974, 5 April 1972.

22 Hartrick, *Drawing*, p. 60; Paul Hills, interviewed 11 June 1991.

23 Hartrick, *Drawing*, p. 66.

24 To *The Times* draft [1951]; MS draft 'Note on Ms' n.d. [c. 1942].

25 Edward Hodgkin to the author, 26 January 1988; Edward Hodgkin, interviewed 1 September 1987; Harman Grisewood, interviewed 5 June 1986; Morag Bulbrook, interviewed 28 June 1988.

26 DJ, 'Life for Jim Ede', typescript 5 September 1935; Eileen Chanin and Steven Miller, *The Art and Life of Weaver Hawkins* (Roseville, New South Wales: Craftsman House, 1995), p. 20.

27 DJ notes for his psychotherapist n.d. [1948]; DJ MS frag. n.d.; to René Hague, 21 October 1963; to Saunders Lewis, April 1971.

CHAPTER 2

ENLISTMENT, TRAINING, EMBARKATION

On 5 August 1914, David Jones was delivered from his anxiety about earning a living as an artist. The front page of *The Times* consisted entirely of the headline:

BRITAIN
AT WAR

Throughout the day, he bought half a dozen editions of various newspapers.[1] History had overtaken the present, and he intended to be part of history.

He wanted to enlist in a Welsh regiment and he had wanted to ride a horse since the age of four, when he had seen a column of cavalry on recruitment parade at the start of the Second Boer War. So he went to the recruitment office of the Royal Welsh Yeomanry at the Inns of Court. The recruiting officer, a major, wore a single eye-glass and was so short and fat that he seemed perfectly round. Jones said he hoped the war would last till Christmas. The major said it would last till Christmas 1918 or '19 and then asked whether Jones or anyone in his family had ridden a horse. Jones said no. The major asked, 'Are you Welsh?' Jones said, 'My father is.' The major then advised him against the Yeomanry, where 'horses receive better treatment than men', and suggested instead the Royal Welch Fusiliers. Jones left discouraged. He never would learn to ride a horse and would always regret it, but he would also always be grateful to the spherical major for putting him off the cavalry.[2]

Anxious that his son join a Welsh regiment, his father wrote, without David knowing, to the Chancellor of the Exchequer, David Lloyd George, who was trying to raise a Welsh Army Corps of two

7. 'from W David
Jones Llandudno
1915'

divisions, one of which would contain a London-Welsh battalion. The
letter was passed to a recruiting officer who replied on 17 September
that the battalion was not yet constituted but was taking applica-
tions for enlistment, and enclosing a badge for David Jones to wear
to an address by the Chancellor at Queen's Hall on Saturday the 19th.
He went and he heard Lloyd George compare 'little Wales' to 'little
Belgium' and 'little' Serbia and announce:

I should like to see a Welsh Army in the field. I should like to see the race who faced the Normans for hundreds of years in their struggle for freedom, the race that helped to win the battle of Crécy, the race that fought for a generation under Glendower against the greatest captain in Europe – I should like to see that race give a good taste of its quality in this struggle. And they are going to do it.

(Lloyd George's oratorical panache and his reference to Crécy suggest that his style may inform the great, rhetorically heightened boast by Dai Greatcoat at the heart of *In Parenthesis* (pp. 79–84), a boast delivered by a soldier who shares the politician's first name.) This was one of three occasions on which Jones heard Lloyd George speak.*³

Jones sent in his application and waited but by the end of October was impatient. Many of his friends had enlisted, and he feared missing his chance. In August, Harold Hawkins had joined the Territorials – the Queen's Westminster Rifles, 1st Battalion of the 16th County of London Regiment – so Jones went to their recruiting station behind St Paul's Cathedral. There he spoke with an unfriendly Cockney sergeant who, when he said he wanted to join the Territorials, replied, 'The Territorials be blowed! This is the bloody Army.' Put off by the man's manner and determined to choose his regiment, Jones turned away.⁴ In September, Frank Medworth enlisted in the East Surrey Regiment.

---

*The second occasion, in the spring of the following year, is mentioned later in this chapter. The third was a visit to the gallery of the House of Commons 'as a young man' in which he noticed that, as Lloyd George spoke, the MPs in the front bench sat, some of them asleep, with their feet up, in spats, against the railing where the mace was – 'just like a drawing in *Punch.*' He would always admire Lloyd George but with reservations, as 'a charming man' (though he could not understand what women saw in him) but unscrupulous, as in his speeding up demobilisation just before the first post-war election. He admired most his ability to 'give his imagination uninhibitedly to the future and let it play, with the result that he had an accuracy of prediction that the custom-bound and those with vested interests were incapable of.' In this sense at least he was not time-bound and therefore resembles Dai Greatcoat, the archetypal soldier who 'never dies' (*IP* 79–84).

On 12 November, Jones went to Duke's Road off Euston Road to enlist in the Artists' Rifles – the London regiment of the 28th (County of London) Reserve Battalion. He filled out the forms and was examined by a doctor named Goodbody, who rejected him as physically unfit 'on account of deficient chest measurement'. Disappointed, he returned home to find a letter announcing that the London Welsh battalion now existed and inviting him to enlist at once. To increase his chest measurement, he donned running shorts and jogged through the streets of Brockley and Lewisham. While jogging, he noticed that the name plate of 'Berlin Road' had been ripped off and temporarily replaced with 'Canada Avenue'.[5] War posters were everywhere, encouraging his exertions, which were, however, futile.

A passage in a manuscript draft of *In Parenthesis* may offer a glimpse of the family at this time:

> One night at supper, his father, pushing his cocoa a little toward the centre of the table, folding his Daily Newspaper in four and resting it upon the cheese-dish, . . . calling the family's attention with a certain solemnity that gave dignity and a momentary return of hierarchy and function to that board, which normally reflected nothing of these things, he began to read,
>
> 'What will you lack, sonny, what will you lack,
> When the girls line up the street
> Shouting their love to the lads to come back
> From the foe they rushed to beat?
>
> Will you send a strangled cheer to the sky
> And grin till your cheeks are red?
> But what will you lack when your mate goes by
> With a girl who cuts you dead?
>
> Where will you look, sonny, where will you look,
> When your children yet to be

Clamour to learn of the part you took
In the War that kept men free?

Will you say it was naught to you if France
Stood up to her foe or bunked?
But where will you look when they give the glance
That tells you they know you funked?

How will you fare, sonny, how will you fare
In the far-off winter night,
When you sit by the fire in an old man's chair
And your neighbours talk of the fight?

Will you slink away, as it were from a blow,
Your old head shamed and bent?
Or say – I was not with the first to go,
But I went, thank God, I went?

Why do they call, sonny, why do they call
For men who are brave and strong?
Is it naught to you if your country fall,
And Right is smashed by Wrong?

Is it football still and the picture show,
The pub and the betting odds,
When your brothers stand to the tyrant's blow,
And England's call is God's!'

Widely used at this time to shame men into enlisting, this verse by Harold Begbie affected the young listener with 'a double-twist'.* It moved Jones because he was patriotic, motivated by a sense of

*The manuscript includes only part of the first stanza, which the poet inaccurately remembers as: 'What will you lack sonny. / What will you lack / When the girls line up the street / And say he was so young.'

duty instilled during his Victorian childhood and his time at Brockley Road School. He was strongly moved by a widely distributed poster enjoining the viewer to 'REMEMBER LOUVAIN!' In August the Germans had razed the city, executing civilians without provocation and burning its great medieval library. On 20 September, German artillery shelled Reims Cathedral. He wanted to help rescue Belgium, to protect France, to restore freedom. He shared a widespread feeling of duty to save western civilization. Although he would never have conceived of it in these terms, he wanted to participate in an immense, international enactment of the saviour-myth. The same altruism motivated most who enlisted – a zeal heightened by a frenzy of propaganda.[6] By Christmas the English press was portraying Germans as barbarian Huns without Christian virtue or human feeling. Until they were defeated, it was claimed, western culture was in jeopardy.

Propaganda focused on the occupation of Belgium, which was brutal, but also generated false accounts of Germans smashing babies against walls, commercially recycling corpses, crucifying Canadians on hayricks (why, he later wondered, on haystacks of all things!) and sodomising nuns.* Newspapers played up the approaching centenary of the Battle of Waterloo in order to associate the current campaign against 'tyranny' with the previous century's heroic efforts against Napoleon. At this time, Jones acquired and read a copy of W. H. Fitchett's *Wellington's Men, Some Soldier Autobiographies* (1900), a collection of extracts from letters of British and French soldiers. It allowed him imaginative access, at least, to the exertions so far denied him, though the vividness of the accounts increased his frustration at inability to enlist.‡ By the new year, recruiting-needs forced relaxation of physical requirements so that, to his great relief, his chest

---

* As a result of discovering after the war that such reports were lies, he would never again trust the press during wartime.

‡ Fifty years later he would reread this book and, from the perspective of an ex-serviceman, be impressed by the power of its factual memories in contrast to subsequent fictional 'improvements'. For example, he thought Wellington's actual words, 'Now, Maitland, now's y'r time' much more believable and more moving than 'Up, Guards, and at them' (MS frag. n.d., c.1965).

measurement (which remained stubbornly unchanged) was no longer inadequate. On 2 January 1915, at the London Welsh recruiting office in Holborn Hall in Gray's Inn Road, he enlisted, receiving his number, 22579, a smallpox vaccination, and his Army Pay Book, in which he listed his mother as his next of kin. For occupation he gave 'Art Student', for religion 'CE', and for his age, exuberantly, '19 2/13'. He signed up for the duration of the war at two shillings per day.[7] He was now a private in the regiment in which commissions were held, in other battalions, by Robert Graves and Siegfried Sassoon, neither of whom he would meet during the war since they were officers and did not socialise with privates.

In the first weeks of January, he continued living at home, each day taking the train up to town, going usually to Hyde Park for infantry-training, which consisted largely of military drill. He and the other recruits wore brown quasi-military greatcoats and used walking-sticks and brooms for rifles. He found drill difficult, tedious and demoralising. One evening after training on Parliament Hill in Hampstead Heath, he was walking away dejectedly in fog and drizzle when one of two passing Cockney girls said to him, 'God bless you, I'd be a soldier too if I had a handle to me belly.' He nearly kissed her.[8]

Before long he joined the 15th Battalion (London Welsh) of the 113th Brigade of the Royal Welch Fusiliers (23rd Foot) of the 38th (Welsh) Division at Llandudno on the north coast of Wales. Stationed there under the command of Lieutenant-Colonel J. C. Bell, formerly of the Central Indian Horse, the battalion had begun recruitment too late to attract most eligible London Welshmen, so membership had been opened to non-Welshmen. As a result, most of the recruits were Cockneys, though there were also a few middle-class Englishmen, some of them, like Jones, of Welsh descent. Except for the Colonel and the Medical Officer, all officers were Welsh. Jones was in the second section of the sixth platoon in B Company. There were ten men in his section, twenty in his platoon (in which he was one of several Joneses), 118 in his company, and about 500 in the battalion.[9]

Beginning with basic training, the war was, for him, an immersion in a rich mixture of Welsh and English languages, accents, idioms, and dispositions. The language he mostly heard was Cockney, the vernacular of the army, its rough poetic idiom a product entirely of aural imagination – unlike the Welsh, many of the Cockneys did not read. He would later say that his Cockney companions might have had for their motto a reversal of the tag *suaviter in modo fortiter in re*, for they were harsh in manner, gentle in deeds. Cockney became part of his own idiom, including its common obscenities – 'sod', 'bugger', and 'fuck' in all of their variations, such as 'sodding', 'buggeration', 'fucking', 'fuck all', 'would you be-fucking-lieve it'. Army Cockney would influence his speech for the rest of his life and be, he later said, a 'potent influence' on his writing. The other three battalions of the 113th Brigade, also stationed at Llandudno, had been recruited entirely in North Wales.[10] Over three-quarters Welsh, this would be his nomadic home in the coming years, a travelling league of tribes, twelve infantry battalions within the 38th (Welsh) Division. A widely registered analogy with the Twelve Tribes of Israel would underlie Old Testament allusions in *In Parenthesis*.

Llandudno, where he joined his unit, was essentially a Victorian resort-town of whitewashed hotels and covered promenades. Above it loomed the headland of the Great Orme, rising, like so many Welsh hills, closer than seems possible to the nearer flatness. Beneath it the town spread eastward in a crescent along its bay towards the Little Orme. The new recruits were billeted two to a room in the lodging houses not occupied by civilians (mostly from Lancashire) on holiday.[11] From here he sent a postcard of himself to his parents. In the photograph he stands in his dress hat and greatcoat, slightly hunched forward, with a dreamy, unsoldierly expression on his face (fig. 7).

Along with all those in training, he began his day at dawn with a two-mile run and drilled and marched for most of the rest of the day. Sometimes they went on operations in the mountains behind Conwy, eating a lunch of haversack rations in the open countryside. He did platoon drill on Llandudno's two-mile-long esplanade. Except for those assigned to guard-duty, work ended for the day at 5 p.m, unless they practised night attacks on the Great Orme.[12] Otherwise, evenings were for relaxing and socialising until lights-out at 10. The men attended concerts and entertainments at half-price. On Sundays they were paraded for worship to the Anglican church in Trinity Square.

He was billeted in a lodging house in Church Walks. One of his room-mates was Harry Marks, a bandsman who played the bass drum, smoked cigars, and drank whisky. At night he regularly entered the room saying, 'Gounod, Gounod – what a musician, and always drunk, thank God.' He refused to put out his cigar before going to bed.

8. 'billets in Ch. Walks Llandudno Harry Marks of the Band very drunk with pinned on "Iron Cross" spring 1915'

Fearing he would set fire to his mattress, Jones stayed awake and when he thought him asleep tiptoed over to remove the cigar, but Marks 'always' heard him approaching and clung steadfastly to it. One evening he returned very drunk and sank into a stupor sitting upright. As a joke, someone pinned an inked-black cardboard German Iron Cross to his chest, and Jones drew the result in profile (fig. 8). Later, in France, he noticed that Marks seemed insensitive to hardship and to the suffering of those around him, but then, like Gounod, 'he was always drunk'.[13]

Other billet mates were an east-end Cockney Jew named Lazarus Black and middle-class Arthur Pritchard-Williams. Black was a former furniture salesman in Gray's Inn Road (see *IP* 155) who developed a warm affection for Jones, which was not fully returned. About him, Jones later said, 'he attached himself to me'. Pritchard-Williams aspired to become a dentist, exchanged postcard-photographs with Jones, and would remain his friend through the early months in France.[14] Jones drew one of his billet mates playing cards (fig. 9)

The men of the brigade were stationed by turns at guard houses along the seven miles of narrow coastal road from Degannwy to the bandstand at Llandudno. Most of the guard houses were on the seaward side of the road skirting the lower bulk of the Great Orme's Head and gave shelter from the strong, continuous cold wind off the Irish Sea. Sentries were stationed there to watch for enemy submarines in the approaches of the Conwy Estuary. The U-boat threat was real. In January, submarines passing from the direction of Anglesey sank three steamers after shelling an airship shed on the Lancashire coast. The sentries were unarmed, however, and Jones wondered what they 'were supposed to do in the event of seeing in the pitch dark waters a German periscope'.[15]

Often he stood watch at one of the sequestered posts beneath the white cliffs of the Great Orme. At midnight under the stars, the waves crashing below, he gazed into the darkness and daydreamed. He was a soldier in a Welsh division defending North Wales, the home of his father's ancestors, the land of the house of Gwynedd, which had ruled

9. 'Spring 1915 at Llandudno billets in Church Walks'

from the time of the Roman-Briton Cunedda Wledig to thirteenth-century Llywelyn ap Gruffydd, the last Welsh prince, whom he had read about in *The Welsh People* and whose death in a wood at Builth on 11 December 1282 he would privately commemorate for the rest of his life. Llandudno was named for its sixth-century saint, Tudno, a contemporary of Maelgwn, a great-grandson of Cunedda. Nearby to the south at Degannwy was a fortress of Maelgwn, originally the Arx Decantorum. Jones had read about Maelgwn in *The Welsh People* and in Gildas, who called him, for his evil deeds, 'Maglocunus, the island dragon'. Coming to North Wales was for Jones an affirmation of ancestral identity, and this included one-eighth of him (on his mother's side) that was Italian. For centuries the defenders of this land had been Romans, with whom, as a soldier, he felt considerable affinity. He would later say of himself and his fellow enlisted men, 'We were about as poorly paid as the Roman army.' On one occasion, on the west side of the Great Orme, while a sergeant harangued him for some infraction or inefficiency, he stood in rapture, gazing past the angry N.C.O. to the massive ranks of the Snowdonian range fronting the sea in lateral sunlight along distant Beaumaris Bay and the Menai Strait.[16] There are few such sights in all the world, and none, for him, so charged with historical imagination.

For a while he was stationed at the lighthouse beside the coastal road on the northern slope of the Great Orme, where a field gun was installed to fire on U-boats. He loved the view from here – the sunsets were the best he had ever seen. There was a lighthouse keeper's daughter, but she was unfriendly and seemed to him in perpetual fear of rape.[17]

On St David's Day, a Sunday, Lloyd George visited Llandudno. Jones attended a united service in the Pier Pavilion at which the 200-voice brigade choir sang *Aberystwyth*, *Crug y Bar*, and *Hyfrydol*. In the afternoon, he was among the 5,000 of the First Brigade of the Welsh Army Corps parading on the promenade in the cold wind and rain. They were inspected by the Chancellor and Douglas Haig, the Commander-in-Chief of the Western Front. Soaked to the skin but with rapt attention, Jones listened as Lloyd George, his hair and cape blowing in the wind, delivered his famous speech about tearing the 'ramshackle' Austro-Hungarian Empire 'limb from limb' with the help of 'the Russian steam-roller'. Jones felt inspired while listening but when reading the speech in the papers a few days later was dismayed to find it 'appalling bloody tripe'.[18]

He stayed in North Wales long enough to feel the weather grow warm and see the wild flowers bloom. By May he and his companions had learned to perform with precision and were participating in brigade field days and staff rides.

One sunny spring day he was part of a working party sent into the Creuddyn Peninsula west of Llandudno. There, after practising digging trenches, they were photographed (fig. 10). At the back, top-

10. *[on reverse] 'Working Party, Creuddyn Peninsula, 1915'*

most on a pile of dirt, Jones stands, small but muscular after seven months of hard exercise.

He hated the endless drill, the parade-ground renunciation of personality, the springing to attention, the marching, the saluting, the presenting arms, right wheel, left wheel, the bullying and insults. He would always consider himself 'incompetent as a "parade soldier"' and confided late in life that he had difficulty telling his right hand from his left. He marvelled that he never incurred a penalty for blunders during drill, parade, or inspection. He also disliked fatigue-duties. He would later say that 'the army itself was frightful', and that he hated his year of training, which was almost always boring.[19]

Yet there were consolations. The army freed him from practical anxieties and difficult choices. All was determined from above, down to the time of going to bed and the manner of lacing of boots. And, when off duty, he was able to visit Llandrillo-yn-Rhos, which was only five miles away. As a child he had gone there for several holidays to visit his cousins Effie and Gladys Tozer. He had played with them on

11. 'Winchester Oct 1915
Winnall Down Camp'

the shore of Colwyn Bay, within sight of a large fishing weir made of
thick wattled fencing secured in a bank of stones. It had been built by
monks in the twelfth century for salmon fishing and had been
repaired and used continually ever since. Jones had loved the look of
its rough wattling. But since then the weir had been damaged by a ship
running aground, and visiting now, he was sad to see it 'much decayed'
with only a few uprights visible at low tide.[20]

He joined in when the marching Cockneys of his battalion belted
out 'Hullo, hullo, who's your lady friend' and other music-hall songs

12. 'Huts Winnal[l] Down Winchester Oct 26th 1915'

of Fred Karno's Army, but with no illusions about the quality of the singing. He was convinced that Englishmen cannot sing. In contrast, the Welsh sang beautifully in harmony. The difference 'was staggering', but he seldom heard Welshmen sing, since the few Welsh in his battalion were not Welsh-speaking and, in the other battalions of the brigade, they 'tended to sing in small groups, & rather guardedly, among themselves – a secret people'. He wondered what they thought of the 'rancorous vulgarity' of the English songs and English singing.[21]

His chief consolation was social. He met friends in the evenings in pubs. If he had not been a beer-drinker in art school, he became one now. The fellowship he experienced within the simplified regimen of army life constituted a unified culture, in relation to which he would later gauge all others. It was the purest, warmest comradeship that most men would ever experience. It would perhaps lend emotional force to his later yearning for a larger integral culture he could not hope to find in the modern civilian world.

If his battalion was almost entirely Cockney, his brigade was

13. 'Huts Winnall Down
Winchester Oct 26 1915'

mostly Welsh and provided what would be his most extensive and intimate experience of the Welsh nation. He now sometimes heard spoken Welsh and the centuries-old Welsh English of Shakespeare's Fluellen. Jones's sergeant-major – also named Jones, a pedantic Boer-war veteran with a large moustache – was 'exactly like' Fluellen except that, instead of 'the disciplines of the wars', he spoke of 'the exigencies of the situation'. For the first time, David Jones got to know what he would later call 'that kind of Welshman little known to the English – silent and without any of the exterior enthusiasm of the supposed "Celt", large of body, kindly, but a terrible disciplinarian'. The ordinary Welsh foot soldiers were, he found, 'pedantic in their rebelliousness', resenting any officer who was, as they put it, 'an ass, whorson vague in his orders'.[22] They had a unique tenor of imagination and expressed

14. 'Salisbury Plain Oct 1915 Lark Hill during musketry course'

themselves peculiarly in English. During the war, Jones heard this joke, which he enjoyed retelling:

> Someone says to a Welshman, 'Oh I hear you've had an accident in
>   the mines.'
> 'It wasn't an accident', replies the Welshman. 'It was an explosion.'
> 'But surely the explosion was an accident.'
> 'Oh no, no.'
> 'What's the difference?'
> 'When you have an accident, well there you are, but with an
>   explosion, where are you?'[23]

In the army, his earlier romantic feeling for Wales gained variegated realistic definition.

It is hard to imagine people less like each other than the Welsh and Cockneys, the former then largely rural, the latter entirely urban. One aspect of the contrast was differing grasps of history. The Welsh had a living sense of their past, and for them it was long. If an Englishman knew any history, it was of England since the Renaissance. For the Welsh, history began before the time of Arthurian legend in the late

15. *'Lark Hill, Salisbury Plain 1915'*

phases of Roman Britain. Jones was chiefly interested in what the Welshman knew and the Englishman didn't.

In August 1915, the entire brigade moved south by train to an immense camp north of Winchester on top of Winnall Down. There they joined the other brigades of the 38th (Welsh) Division, of which only his battalion was not Welsh. They lived in wooden huts and congregated in the evenings in recreation rooms. On the assumption that the war would return to the mobility of the months before the battle of the Marne, they trained in the countryside for open warfare.

On Winnall Down, he first heard 'the drummed and fifed Long Reveille', which he found 'very moving' despite 'the atrocious time of day'. Here also he used to 'adore lying in an army hut while some bugler played lights out'.[24]

One Sunday morning, as Anglicans and Catholics were detailed to

16. David Jones, 1915

go to church and 'other religions' were given fatigue duty, a sergeant named Morgan assigned Lazarus Black the unpleasant job of shovelling coal, adding, 'That's for crucifying Jesus Christ.' Jones thought it very funny that anyone could say that, as if living early in the first century AD.[25] He may have missed the irony of Jesus himself being a Jew.

In September, all the battalions of the Division were inspected, found fit for combat, and began preparing to leave for France at the end of November. They began musketry training in October on Lark Hill, though the rifles were substandard and there were not yet enough for everyone. The men were granted pre-embarkation leave, and he went home to say goodbye. His parents had several photographs taken of him, as an unspoken precaution against never seeing him again (fig. 16).[26]

While on leave, he visited Camberwell Art School and spoke with his former teacher, A. S. Hartrick, who at fifty had twice tried unsuccessfully to enlist and was making lithographs for war posters. He asked Jones to make a drawing for publication in *The Graphic*, the illustrated weekly of which Hartrick was art editor. Near the end of November, Jones sent a drawing, which was photographically reproduced in the issue of 11 December 1915 (fig. 17). In block capitals, obscure in the lower left corner, is the signature, 'W DAVID JONES 1915'. This is the first of five drawings he contributed to the *Graphic* during the war. Their idealism would not, in later years, suit his mature understanding of world politics. Fifty-eight years later he would say to me and William Blissett (adding, 'I have never told anyone else') that he had published this drawing in the *Illustrated London News*. Because of his reticence and his misremembering the name of the publication, this and other wartime drawings published in *The Graphic* have not, since their first publication, been attributed to him until now.

Sentimentally conventional, this drawing depicts a medieval knight with laurel crowning his helmet, the suggestion of a nimbus at his head, and the words 'Pro Patria' on his shield. He holds his sword handle-up, so that it evokes a cross, in a gesture of devotion

while guarding fallen or sleeping British soldiers – the foremost of them based on the second figure in the sketch Jones had drawn on Salisbury Plain in October (fig. 18). The knight's statuesque erectness contrasts with the crumpled figure at his feet and the chaotic background in which an aeroplane careers over leaning telegraph poles, a howitzer, and the wreckage of battle. Visually, the knight and his sword stabilise chaos. His

17. Pro Patria, The Graphic,
11 December 1915

prominence and that of the foremost sleeper suggests a symbolic relationship between knight and infantryman, past and present. As this indicates, before going to France Jones saw continuity between medieval chivalry and the devotion of soldiers caught up in messy, unglamorous modern war, with which he was visually familiar through newspaper and magazine photographs. A sense of this continuity would survive experience of combat and influence *In Parenthesis*, where it would, however, be free of political partisanship. Like the soldier in the drawing reproduced in Chapter 1

18. '(Salisbury Plain), Oct. 1915 DJ'

(fig. 5), this knight resembles his creator – they have the same nose and prominent chin. Noticing the resemblance, Hartrick gave the picture the ambiguous caption, 'The Soldier as Cartoonist'. While his shield proclaims patriotism, the knight guards not his country but his companions, an indication that the meaning of military service had already shifted in emphasis for Jones, as it did for most if not all soldiers, from love of country to love of comrades. This aspect of the drawing, too, has important thematic affinity with *In Parenthesis* (see especially pp. 51–5, where Private John Ball stands night-sentry). The depiction of Jones-as-knightly-sentinel reflects his experience standing night-watch over sleeping men during his year of training. The image of himself protecting sleepers against chaos also prefigures his poetic and artistic devotion in later years to retrieving and pre-serving endangered elements of western culture – as in his final poem, 'The Sleeping Lord'.

He was back in camp on Winnall Down when the full complement

19. 'Salisbury Plain Oct 15'

of their rifles finally arrived in mid-November. His battalion went immediately to ranges on nearby Salisbury Plain for musketry instruction. They were billeted in large circular bell-tents on Lark Hill at the northern edge of the plain. Each morning an orderly corporal opened the flap of the tent to wake them, and through the opening he saw, about two miles away across the plain, Stonehenge. He would confess to 'not finding' it 'very impressive' at the time, though he liked Constable's picture of it, and his morning-vision of the distant stone circle later entered his paintings – *Vexilla Regis* (1947), for example, and *The Paschal Lamb* (1951).[27]

The musketry instructors were Scots, rigidly, pedantically efficient – a characteristic he respected but disliked and from now on associated with Scotsmen in general. He admired his perfectly balanced Lee-Enfield Short rifle and for two weeks he practised nothing but musketry. He learned 'rapid fire', a controlled volley of ten to fifteen rounds. He attempted 'independent fire', shooting as fast as possible for as long as possible, which he found differed little from rapid fire since he could not fire beyond ten rounds quickly without the magazine jamming, nor did he ever meet anyone who could. At Camberwell, Hartrick had spoken of drawing as learning 'how to shoot' and taught them to 'shoot straight'. In Jones's case, this turned out to be more than a metaphor – with the trained hand-eye co-ordination of an artist, he shot accurately and, at the end of two weeks, was rated 'a first class shot'.[28] An even better marksman, his friend Arthur Pritchard-Williams (the proto-dentist) was made a sniper.

Shortly before going overseas, B Company of the 15th Battalion had its photograph taken (fig. 20). Jones is the fourth from the right in the fourth row. To his right is Pritchard-Williams. Above the big drum, with protruding ears, is Colonel J. C. Bell; to his right, Captain Jack Edwards. Jones also had his photograph taken solo, 'just before going to France' (his note on the reverse of the photograph) on what

20. B Company, 15th Battalion (London Welsh) Royal Welch Fusiliers (23rd Foot), 1915; Jones is in third long row, fourth from (the viewer's) right

21. Arthur Pritchard-Williams and David Jones [detail of fig. 14]

appears to be Winnall Down, in dress uniform and puttees and holding a walking stick (fig. 22).

On 29 November on Crawley Down, the entire Division was reviewed by the Queen and Princess Mary. Rain fell hard throughout the ceremony, which was, for Jones, 'an exceedingly depressing experience in all respects'.[29]

On 1 December at 5.45 a.m., having padded his shoulders with socks against the bite of knapsack straps (*IP MS*), he scrambled into line and began marching the seventeen miles to the Southampton docks and embarkation. Marching was now a torment because he had developed rheumatism in one foot. He dreaded its worsening in the trenches.[30]

The battalion paraded in rain and passed through sleeping Winchester into open country. Perpendicular, penetrating rain increased with dawn and then fell steadily, increasing the weight they carried. Owing to newly issued hard overseas boots and hard-wool issue socks, the entire column was soon limping. Although the road was straight, confusion among officers about the route lengthened the journey considerably, their incompetence infuriating the men who were forced to stand in full gear, using rifles to prop the weight of packs.

22. '1915 just before going to France'

Small and relatively slight, Jones seemed to others in his battalion to be extremely young. As he struggled beneath the weight of his pack and limped painfully on his rheumatic foot, a platoon-mate carried his rifle for him. On long marches, one or another of them frequently did this, after commiserating, 'Poor little sod.'[31] Not yet at his full height of 5 feet 7 ½ inches, he was smaller than most of the others but carried the same burden – 77 pounds on a dry day, increased as now by rain, which soaked his thick wool greatcoat, to 100 pounds, which was approximately his body-weight.* The battalion arrived at the Southampton docks at 12:30 p.m. They rested in sheds till the afternoon of the next day. At 4:30 p.m. on 2 December, they commenced boarding the *Queen Alexandra*, which departed at 6 p.m., crossing the Channel at night to avoid detection by U-boats.

* His height is recorded in his 1928 passport. Assuming that his civilian clothes fit or nearly fit in 1915, a photo taken of him wearing them on leave in 1917 shows, by the distance of his trouser-cuffs from his shoes, that he grew two to three inches between 1915 and October 1917. From the look of him in photographs, he could not have weighed much more than 100 pounds. The average weight of an infantryman was 138 pounds.

NOTES TO CHAPTER 2

1 To Harman Grisewood, 4 August 1962; DJ, 'Fragments of an Attempted Autobiographical Writing', *Agenda* 12 (Winter–Spring 1975), p. 106; William Blissett recalling visits to DJ in June 1973 in conversation with author.

2 Letter to Bernard Bergonzi, 11 November 1965; DJ in conversation with Blissett and author, 31 August 1972; my notes on Blissett recalling visits to DJ in June 1973; DJ interview by Saunders Lewis (1965) in Michael Alexander's 'David Jones', BBC 2 radio programme 1977; to René Hague, 7 November 1963; *DGC* 27.

3 To Harman Grisewood, 1 January 1964; to Valerie Wynne-Williams, draft 5 April 1962; Lloyd George, *Through Terror to Triumph* (London: Hodder and Stoughton, 1915), p. 13. Soon after it was delivered, the speech was published in its entirety and widely circulated as a pamphlet under two titles: *Through Terror to Triumph* (London: Liberal Publication Dept, 1914), and *Honour and Dishonour* (London: Methuen, 1914). To Harman Grisewood, 4 August 1962; DJ in conversation with Tony Stoneburner, written record 9 June 1966.

4 Chanin and Miller, p. 28; to William Blissett, *The Long Conversation*, pp. 116–7.

5 Certified Notice of Attestation, 12 November 1914; to James Jones, 11 November 1914 (a letter posted in the afternoon in London at this time would have arrived the next day); *DGC* 26; to René Hague, 13 October 1963.

6 *DGC* 26; 'A Soldier's Memories', *Tablet* (16 April 1938), p. 506.

7 Certified Copy of Attestation, 2 January 1915.

8 William Blissett recalling visits to DJ in June 1973 to author; letter draft frag. 1970; Philip Hagreen, interviewed 27 June 1986.

9 To René Hague, 5 November 1964; DJ in conversation with author, 5 June 1971. The numbers in his section and battalion are approximate, based on the numbers in DJ's platoon and company (fig. 20), and they are lower than full strength, which would be 1,000 men per battalion.

10 To Peter Levi, 27 August 1964; DJ, 'Life for Jim Ede' (5 September 1935), second correction of typescript, 3 May 1943; DJ interviewed by Peter Orr, early 1970s; letter to Bernard Bergonzi, 11 November 1965.

11 To Bernard Bergonzi, 11 November 1965.

12 To Valerie Wynne Williams, 6 August 1962.

13 To René Hague, 9–11 June 1974, 7 November 1935.

14 Colin Hughes, *David Jones: The Man Who Was on the Field. In Parenthesis as Straight Reporting* (Manchester: David Jones Society, 1979), p. 9; DJ in conversation with author, 24 August 1972; Arthur Pritchard-Williams to DJ, 15 November 1944.

15 *The Borough of Colwyn Handbook*, ed. Richard E. Baddeley (Colwyn Bay: Borough of Colwyn Environmental Improvement Scheme, 1987), p. 58; to Bernard Bergonzi, 11 November 1965.

16 *Manchester Guardian*, 11 February 1972; letter draft frag. n.d. [1970]; Maurice Bradshaw interviewed by Tony Stoneburner, 1975.

17 Blissett, p. 120.

18 Blissett, p. 71; to Valerie Wynne Williams, 6 August 1962. DJ remembered hearing the

speech 'in the pavilion on the pier at Llandudno' (to René Hague, 11 August 1974) although the *Llandudno Register* reported that it was delivered at nearby Conwy Bay (5 March 1915).

19 To David Blamires, 26 January 1972; DJ interviewed by Peter Orr, early 1970s.

20 Tony Hyne, interviewed June 1985; *The Borough of Colwyn Handbook*, p. 63; to Gwladys Toser, 26 October 1948; to Tony Hyne, 18 May 1972.

21 To Donald Attwater, 10 December 1944; to Harman Grisewood, 9 October 1971; 25 December 1930; letter frag. n.d.

22 DJ interviewed by Peter Orr, early 1970s; to Peter Levi, 29 October 1963; DJ, 'A Soldier's Memories', *Tablet* (16 April 1938), p. 506; to René Hague, 11 August 1974.

23 In the early 1920s he told it to Philip Hagreen, interviewed October 1987.

24 DJ interviewed by Jon Silkin 1971, typescript; Lt. Colonel J. E. Munby, ed., *A History of the 38th (Welsh) Division by the G.S.O.'s I of the Division* (London: Hugh Rees, 1920), dated by DJ July 1929, p. 13; Stanley Honeyman interviewed 21 June 1986; MS draft n.d. [c. 1965].

25 To Valerie Wynne Williams, 11 December 1959; Valerie Wynne Williams to author, 13, 14 February 2006.

26 This photograph was reproduced in an article on Jones in the *Sunday Times Magazine* of 1 July 1976 and subsequently lost. The image is taken from the magazine.

27 Although Munby writes in *A History of the 38th (Welsh) Division*, that rifles arrived in mid-August, an entry in the *War Diary of the 15th Battalion, Royal Welch Fusiliers* indicates mid-November, and the experience of the 15th Battalion was not necessarily that of the others in the division. Colin Hughes writes that the battalions had some sub-standard rifles while in North Wales and that the shortage of rifles persisted until November (p. 9). To Saunders Lewis, April 1971. For most of the details of the movements of the battalion in this chapter, I rely on the battalion war diary. To Petra Tegetmeier, 6–7 September 1970; to Richard and Juliet Shirley-Smith, 17 August 1961.

28 Stanley Honeyman to author, 20 June 1986; to Harman Grisewood, 12 December 1966; Blissett, p. 81; A.S. Hartrick, *A Painter's Pilgrimage*, p. 12; to John Roberts of Ganymed Press, frag. n.d. [1961].

29 DJ's annotations to his copy of Munby, p. 14.

30 To Valerie Wynne Williams, 5 April 1963.

31 Unnamed fellow battalion member to DJ, 1 July 1937. I paraphrase words addressed to Bobby Saunders (*IP* 6), whom David Jones modelled on himself and who, in early drafts, had been initially kept from enlisting by insufficient chest expansion. Alice Hyne in conversation with Stanley Honeyman, interviewed 14 June 1991.

CHAPTER 3

RICHEBOURG SECTOR

The crossing was rough. Seven hours after departing, the battalion arrived in Le Havre, disembarked in the rain at 7 a.m., and marched to a rest-camp outside town. That evening they marched to the railway station and, at 9 p.m., boarded a train travelling north to Blendecques. They arrived at 6 in the morning at the station-yard near St Omer where they emerged into the still-falling rain. In northern France everything man-made differed slightly from its counterpart in England. Villages were smaller, the roofs of the red-brick houses at a slightly sharper incline. Instead of hedges, pollarded willows and long poplars lined the roads.

Considered insufficiently trained, the troops were ordered not to the front but to two more weeks of training. In the rain they marched to the village of Warne, a mile south of Rocquetoire. Here they billeted in farm out-buildings. The farm where Jones stayed was pleasant, with a family, a dog, chickens, an orchard, a stream from which to fetch washing water, and a rectangular field bordered by bushes where they drilled.[1] They remained here from the 4th to the 19th – all this time the cold rain continuing, more rain than in any December for 39 years.

Each day, wearing waterproof capes over greatcoats, they did short route-marches through the saturated countryside and platoon-drill and arms-drill behind billets in the rectangular field. Now with rifles to fix bayonets to, they practised bayonet-drill properly. On especially wet days, they assembled in a barn to hear lectures by the battalion officers, all regular army. Speaking on strategy, Colonel Bell gave them the benefit of his long experience with the Gurkhas. The men were fond of him and considered him quite old – he was in his early fifties. The Adjutant, Captain Thomas Elias, had been a lawyer and wore thick spectacles. Calm, efficient, dapper, remembered by Jones as a 'jolly nice chap', he narrated the history of the regiment, revealing that the 23rd Foot was first raised to fight for William III, 'Dutch William', at the Battle of the Boyne in 1690 – an origin that made Jones, who was pro-Irish, 'bloody angry'. A bombing officer told them how their predecessors had improvised bombs out of tin cans and scrap metal and how fortunate they now were to have the new Mills bomb (the modern grenade shaped like a small pineapple). The most popular lectures were those by the medical officer, 'Doc Day', a specialist in tropical diseases. He spoke vividly and comically about sexual hygiene and venereal disease – it was the frankest sexual talk that Jones had heard. According to official army policy, sexual intercourse was natural, almost a practical necessity. This was a radical departure from the prudery of his lower-middle-class Victorian upbringing. He would commemorate this doctor, 'who glossed his technical discourses with every lewdness, whose heroism and humanity reached toward sanctity' (*IP* 13).[2]

In the evenings they congregated at an estaminet, a farmhouse converted into a café presided over by the lady of the house. Here, in small groups, they sat at circular marble or painted metal tables drinking grenadine, grey coffee in glasses, sour cheap red wine, or light French beer which they were convinced was watered. At night they slept in thick dry straw.

The men were issued sleeveless sheep-skin jackets, which delighted Jones. Worn with the wool outside, grey, white, and black, they lent variety to khaki, gave rough splendour to drab, ill-fitting uniforms, and were warm. In them, the men looked like Greek bandits – though usually, and always on the march, they wore them under greatcoats.

On the 19th after reveille at 4.30 a.m., they donned full packs and divided among themselves paraphernalia belonging in common to each platoon, such as picks, periscopes, and wire-cutters. They boarded grey-painted London buses for La Gorgue, near Estaires. On the way, they saw for the first time ammunition dumps, field hospitals, ordnance workshops and supply depots. From La Gorgue, in the late afternoon, they proceeded on foot between tall poplars down the

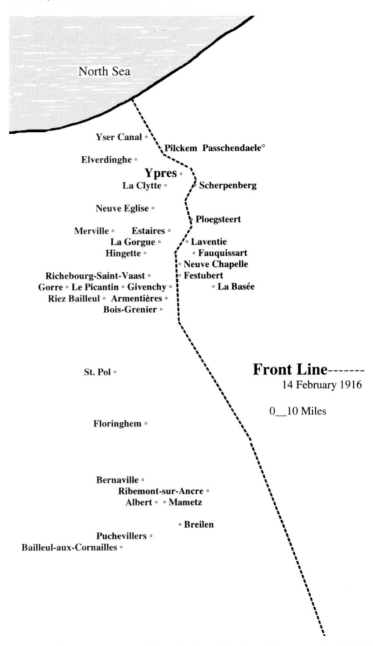

North Sea

Yser Canal ◦
⚬ Pilckem Passchendaele◦
Elverdinghe ◦
Ypres ◦
La Clytte ◦   ⚬ Scherpenberg

Neuve Eglise ◦
◦ Ploegsteert
Merville ◦   Estaires ◦
La Gorgue ◦   ⚬ Laventie
Hingette ◦   ◦ Fauquissart
◦ Neuve Chapelle
Richebourg-Saint-Vaast ◦   ◦ Festubert
Gorre ◦ Le Picantin ◦ Givenchy ◦   ◦ La Basée
Riez Bailleul ◦ Armentières ◦
Bois-Grenier ◦

St. Pol ◦   **Front Line**-------
14 February 1916

0___10 Miles
Floringhem ◦

Bernaville ◦
Ribemont-sur-Ancre ◦
Albert ◦ ◦ Mametz

◦ Breilen
Puchevillers ◦
Bailleul-aux-Cornailles ◦

23. Map: the Western Front, including locations where David Jones served or sketched

64

straight, paved Estaires-La Bassée road. They heard the coughing of artillery and watched aeroplanes high above machine gunning each other. Jones and the others in his battalion passed ruined farm buildings and crossed newly filled-in shell-holes in the road. Some of the trees flanking the road were broken, and they came to freshly gaping holes. Now within range of long-range enemy artillery, they began marching by platoons in 'artillery formation' to minimise casualties from any incoming fire.[3] They turned right, onto a smaller road and a mile later reached Riez Bailleul, a cluster of small farms. Here they joined a battalion of the Third Grenadier Guards for instruction during their first two weeks in the trenches.

Near a heavy artillery battery, as he was about to enter a barn where they were to rest till nightfall, Jones's lieutenant asked, 'Have you a match, Jones?' 'Oh yes', he replied forgetting protocol, 'I have some here.' Without insisting on being sirred, the lieutenant took one, lit his cigarette, and – something officers seldom did – returned the box. As the lieutenant departed, Jones's sergeant, who had overheard the exchange, began to lecture Jones on the proper manner of addressing commissioned officers but abruptly fell silent and withdrew into the barn. Jones stood transfixed in the small farmyard, sensing it coming – a long-range heavy shell. It struck in a screaming apotheosis of violence 50 yards away. He was profoundly shaken. Afterwards he saw the gaping shell-hole and noticed dirt and turnip-sap spattering the breech-block of a nearby field-gun. For him, that explosion tore time in two, dividing his early years of life from all to follow. He would later poetically recreate the explosion very much as he experienced it:

> Out of the vortex, rifling the air it came – bright, brass-shod, Pandoran; with all-filling screaming the howling crescendo's up-piling snapt. The universal world, breath held, one half second, a bludgeoned stillness. Then the pent violence released a consummation of all burstings out; all sudden up-rendings and rivings-through – all taking-out of vents – all barrier-break-

ing – all unmaking. Pernitric begetting – the dissolving and splitting of solid things. (*IP* 24)[4]

After dark they resumed their journey towards lights flashing in the eastern sky. It was four miles to the front line, the last three-quarters of a mile through flooded communication trenches. In platoons separated by intervals of 100 yards, they struggled forward in pitch darkness, almost too tired to stay awake. Stumbling near-automatons, each conscious primarily of the weight of his kit, they splashed through slime, following the zigzagging communication trench. (No trench could safely run perpendicular to the direction of enemy fire.) They reached their destination in the firing-trench just east of where the Estaires-La Bassée road ran above ground. They were told to fix bayonets – this was standing orders in the front line – and settled in. Those not assigned to sentry-duty slept.

On 20 December, Jones experienced for the first time the impressive daily ritual of 'stand-to'. A half-hour before dawn all the men in the front trench stood alert, heads and shoulders above ground

24. *'March 1916. Front line trench on La Bassée Front'*

66

in anticipation of an attack. As darkness gave way to daylight and the mist thinned, he saw the world into which he had come – an erratically undulating, primordially quasi-liquid, slate-coloured plain with only barbed wire for vegetation. A hundred and fifty yards ahead was the German firing-trench, in which all of them were also standing-to. After an hour of standing and watching, just before vision across no man's land became clear, he with all the others withdrew underground.

The trench was lined with sandbags filled with dirt or, preferably, clay. The front of the trench (the parapet) was eight feet high. Fires for warmth and cooking burned in petrol drums, ventilated at the

25. '(periscope) early in 1916 place uncertain'

base with bullet holes (fig. 24). Knee-high against the parapet ran a ledge called the fire-step, on which everyone stood at stand-to and sentries stood at night. Made of sandbags elsewhere, the fire-step was made of duck boards here to allow for drainage. 'The fire-step was', Jones later wrote, 'the front-fighter's couch, bed-board, food-board, card-table, workman's bench, universal shelf, the only raised surface on which to set a thing down above water level. . . . The nature, height, & repair of fire-steps were of great moment to the front line soldier, especially before adequate dugouts became customary in all trenches.' During the day, sentries sat or knelt on it as they looked through periscopes (fig. 25) or, when these were in short supply, at reflections in shaving-mirrors attached to fixed bayonets (IP MS). (Often he thought of what passing 'through the looking-glass' might mean here.) Timbers braced the parapet against the back (parados), jammed against revetment frames strung with wire to hold the sandbags against collapse. Trenches were broken by traverses into ten-yard-long fire-bays to limit damage if the enemy occupied a neighbouring fire-bay or if a shell burst in one. (Fire-bays were an innovation of Confederate General James Longstreet at Fredericks-burg just over half a century before.) Long communication trenches zigzagged back from the firing-trench to the support trench and from there to the reserve trench. Life underground was local and close: seldom could you see further than ten yards in any level direction. Moving in the maze of trenches, you were usually aware only of the approximate direction in which you were heading and the general run of the enemy line. In the parados were dugouts, rooms in the earth about five feet long, five feet wide, and six feet high. They were usually crowded, the atmosphere fetid. In them, out of the rain, men played cards, gossiped about the war, and read newspapers. Dugout floors were lower than the bottoms of trenches and usually wet. For safety, their timbered entrances were small and took some agility to sling yourself through. Because there were too few dugouts to sleep in, many men wrapped themselves in groundsheets and snatched what sleep they could while curled up on a fire-step or in cubby holes scooped out of the parados.

Men stood guard for periods of three hours, followed by three hours to sleep, followed in turn by three hours of fatigue duty. Up to a third of the men stood watch during the day, twice that number at night. Night-sentries were ordered to stand with head and shoulders above the parapet because enemy machine-guns were trained just above the ground and it was better to be hit in the chest or shoulder than in the forehead. Often the darkness was broken by Verey lights – bright flares, hissing as they rose to explode and shower down red, white, blue, or green, 'feebly illuminating / the nearer surfaces, pallid shadows / circled with its circling – sunk / spitting, rain-snuffed out' (IP MS). They reminded Jones of fireworks at the Crystal Palace. Night-sentries had to remain still, and before long became unbearably, teeth-chattering cold – the cold kept most sentries awake.

Sentries did not wear packs, and before the cold penetrated, it was a relief to be free of the otherwise perpetual drag on shoulders. (A few months later, all men entering the front line would be allowed to dump packs at Quartermaster Stores.) It was liberating to see above ground in moonlight. Jones later described what he saw:

> Heaped rusted conglomerate tangles, dripping water, like rained-on, iron-briars, tentaculated sprawlings, staked with rigid up-rights rising from fantastique earth undulations. (*IP* MS)

On day-sentry, he saw through a mirror the cook-fires rising from the enemy trench, and a mile beyond, the leafless, broken trees of Biez Wood. Usually, there was nothing much else to see, and sentry-duty was prime time for daydreaming, but it was unnerving in fog, which obscured whatever might be happening immediately in front. For the rest of his life, fog would remind him of the tension it brought him on sentry-duty.[5]

In the firing-trench, he experienced the most vivid and indescribable aspect of trench-life, its smell. To the end of his life he would be able to recall 'the unpleasant smell' of the 'bluish grey slime' of subsoil covering the surface of the shell-torn earth. There were also smells arising from latrines, from shell holes used as latrines, from mildew, from cordite, from wood smoke, from the sweat of unwashed men, from noxious whale-oil grease applied daily to bare feet (waterproofing them to prevent trench-foot, a condition resembling frostbite), from chloride of lime scattered to prevent contagion, and above all from putrefaction. In all seasons, this last was the dominant odour: the sour smell of corpses of mules, horses (in support areas), and men. Digging a trench, a sap or a latrine, men on fatigue regularly encountered human bodies in various stages of decay. Artillery churned up (and further mutilated) corpses. Men smoked to cover a little this stench – though Jones did not much mind it since, he later said, 'it was a natural thing'. He liked 'the absolutely unique smells of engineers' dumps – mainly of rusted wire . . . & newly cut lengths of soft-wood for revetting frames'. Smells varied in pungency and composition depending on your location and the direction of the wind. High-explosive shells released acrid fumes that lingered for a long while. Great foulness was unleashed when a shell hit a latrine. As though determined to add as little as possible to the general odour, he asked his mother to send him a solid stick of eau-de-cologne, which he found 'a jolly useful thing to have'.[6]

His initial experience in the firing-trench ended at 3 p.m. on the 21st, when the battalion withdrew to a support trench. After two days there, they returned to the front line. Apart from extreme discomfort, theirs was a tranquil apprenticeship since heavy rain and the struggle with mud discouraged both sides from heavy firing.

During these weeks, he learned to ignore the roar of the big 'coal-boxes' that fell in the rear and to listen for the brief light piping or humming of smaller shells aimed at trenches. He learned to dread the cough of the heavy trench-mortar which lobbed a shell into a trench with a concussion so strong it could blow a man out of his clothes and blast a trench wide open. He learned to linger when off duty at traverses so that when he heard a mortar shell descending from its high trajectory he could, by leaping round the corner, put a solid barrier between himself and the explosion. There was no point trying to judge the trajectory of a rifle grenade: when you heard its thin hiss you dived into the grey-blue muck and stayed there until after the metallic rip of its bursting. Before long he became a connoisseur of all this fiery modern music, able to distinguish in-coming shells by calibre. He learned to discriminate between the varying orchestrations of a barrage and know when it had not quite attained the status of 'drum fire' – the term for uninterrupted roaring. He learned never to peek over the parapet in daylight since a sniper needed only a half-second to see you and shoot.

He also became proficient at stringing barbed wire. Nearly every night in the front line and in support areas, fatigues went above ground to repair and add to the local entanglements. Noiselessly (no hammering) they twisted corkscrew-tipped stakes into the earth at regular intervals and attached streams of wire. Two men held the heavy roll while others spooled it off. It may have been while stringing wire that he first heard Welshmen of a mining company 'in a sap-head or some such place' singing, very softly, *Sospan Fach*, a rugby football anthem of pots, pans, and billikins. It reminded him of the distant Celtic past, partly by recalling the Welsh saying 'To Gwenhwyvar the pot, to Arthur the pan.'[7]

26. 'washing 1916, La Bassée area'

Although hard and dangerous, he liked this new life better than the empty routine and irksome discipline of the previous year. Only now did anything military acquire meaning. Life also become more relaxed. Camaraderie increased – 'people who could be jolly horrible', he later said, 'were so much nicer to each other' – and this involved all ranks. Even though it was a fearful experience, he 'much preferred being in the line' to being anywhere else in the army.[8]

Christmas Day was mild. In the morning he heard Germans singing carols and Cockneys singing louder to drown them out. The Cockneys sang 'Casey Jones', a song that he particularly liked. Before noon, his battalion went into a rest area behind the line. They zigzagged back through the communication trench and moved overground up the Estaires-La Bassée road, passing Cockney artillerymen straddling muzzles of heavy field-guns and singing carols very badly, their guns, 18 pounders, decorated with garlands.[9]

That afternoon he heard that in the forward trench men from his regiment were meeting Germans in no man's land to exchange food,

71

drink, and cigarettes. This unofficial truce was not as extensive as the now famous one of the previous Christmas. The men had been ordered on Christmas Eve not to fraternise with 'those people'. (How pleased he was whenever orders referred to the enemy as 'those people' or 'his people'.) News of the current truce moved him. He longed to take part in it, but that afternoon artillery fire cancelled peace on earth.[10] It was to be the last Christmas truce of the war and never publicly acknowledged or entered into the historical record – until Jones mentioned it in his second epic-length poem, *The Anathemata* (p. 216).

The novelty of trench-life quickly faded to routine. After morning 'stand-down', there was usually an hour of tacit truce, during which they ate breakfast and drank tea, followed by rifle inspection about 8.30 a.m. Then fatigue parties assembled mostly to repair trenches damaged in the night. The midday meal, usually stew accompanied by tea, was much anticipated because the post (and newspapers and magazines) came with rations.

He read *The Daily Graphic* 'with its full page pictures of the High Command', its assurances 'that the spirit of the troops is excellent / and that the nation proceeds confidently in its knowledge of Victory', articles on 'Fr Vaughan in Brompton Road "urging greater zeal in the matter of killing"', pictures of Miss Lena Ashwell and of the Cheltenham girls, and 'a notice of Mr Belloc lecturing off the Strand'. He also now began reading the *Times Literary Supplement*.[11]

The daily rations distributed at lunchtime included: one pound of meat, a portion of vegetables, bread (inevitably stale), and Ticklers Jam and Dairy-Maid canned butter. There were also army biscuits, sometimes so hard they had to be cracked with a rifle butt. From home some men received King George Chocolates, which most loved, and Maconochie tinned meat-and-vegetables, advertised as 'The Ideal Ration' but extremely greasy and generally considered inedible. Jones once received six tins from his sister, which, one by one, he discus-hurled into no man's land – as if to test the claim of its advertisement, 'a little goes a very long way'. Tea tasted of the chloride of lime used to purify the water and often also of whatever had previously been cooked in the field-cook's vat. Food for privates was inferior to that for officers. Only officers, for example, were allowed to indulge in the regimental tradition of eating leeks on St David's Day. (On that day in 1917, Jones would see a large consignment of leeks on its way to an officer's mess, steal one, wear it tied to his helmet for the rest of the day, and cook it that night for supper.)[12]

More fatigue-parties followed lunch. In the evening loose tea-and-sugar was brought up pre-mixed in a sack (one per section) for supper at 6 p.m. and for the next day's breakfast. At dusk everyone stood-to again for an hour, watching for the enemy as mist rose from flooded shell-holes. Afterwards some men were assigned to sentry-duty, others assigned to fatigues, and others allowed to sleep before their turn at one or the other. This was the routine he would experience for much of the next 39 months.

Fatigues were continual, repetitive, and boring. Deepen this trench, repair that trench, repair this dugout, fill sandbags, dig a sap, sink a latrine, take buckets and empty the latrine, bring up rations, bring up ammunition, bring up barbed wire, bring up sheets of corrugated iron (from a depot that might be two miles away), repair a gap in the wire, add to the wire, deepen this trench, repair that trench. Whether you were in the front line or in support or reserve trenches, there was no relief from fatigues. Fatigues in the front line were worse because you had to carry your rifle in addition to whatever material you had to carry (ch. 6, fig. 48). So aptly named were fatigues that, a month before Jones's arrival, headquarters had decreed in an attempt to improve morale that they were henceforth to be referred to as 'work parties'. But language does not alter by decree, and fatigues remained fatigues.

He was assigned to fatigue duty more often than some since, apart from being a good shot, he had no special skills. He was, and would be for much of the war, one of the ordinary foot-mob, the 'platoon wallahs' who comprised the army's lower class, its labourers. The upper classes consisted of specialist units in the battalion: the Signallers, the bombers, the grenade throwers, the stretcher-bearers (big strong men), the snipers, the machine-gunners, and the 'Suicide Club' who fired trench mortars, which always elicited retaliation. These were sometimes exempt from fatigues and even sentry-duty. He and his kind were not.

Seldom off duty day or night, they were always tired. Chronic weariness sometimes reached the point of torment. Depending on the strength of a company, a man might spend over a week with no more than one hour off duty at a time, and many such interludes had to be spent cleaning rifles. The time between 3.30 a.m. and 'stand-to' was usually quiet, however, and those not on fatigue or standing guard slept then.

Extreme weariness, boredom, occasional hunger and thirst (fear made men thirsty): this was life in the trenches, punctuated by sudden horrific violence and hurried effort, made hateful by rain and mud and, in winter, by almost unbearable cold. The winter of 1915–16 was bitter, sunless and wet, with rain turning to sleet and mud to grey slush. Perpetually wet, they were cold when not huddled round fires. Jones agreed with most who thought the war '*could* not possibly last another winter – no one would "stick it"'.[13] He inherited from his mother sensitivity to the cold, from which, after winters in the trenches, he would suffer for the rest of his life.

After two weeks of permanent saturation, with feet usually ankle-deep in water, the rheumatism in his foot vanished. He had never been (and would never be) so healthy as in the trenches. The sick were not coddled in the army. Men on 'Excused Duty' were almost always assigned to 'Medicine and Duty', which meant that they carried on as usual, with the added nuisance of having to attend daily sick-parade. If you were very ill, and assigned to 'Light Duty', you performed 'any scavenger job going'. Despite the wet cold, he ceased being ill partly because illness brought none of the advantages he had known as a malingering child and partly because fear increased levels of adrenalin, which supercharges the immune system. He would catch cold almost immediately upon returning home on leave, but this was usual among most of the men.[14]

27. *'Richebourg 1916 Spring'*

Life in the trenches was not all bad, if only because opposites intensify each other. There were letters from home, and occasional experiences of being warm, unafraid, not thirsty, not hungry. The pure intensity of such pleasures had been, for him, unknown in civilian life. Sleep (and dreaming) on boards, against sandbags, anywhere, was delectable release. Best of all was rest in reserve billets where, after weeks in cold rain and mud under enemy fire, he had, for several days, dry blankets over straw on a stone floor under a roof – though here senseless military discipline reasserted itself.

There were also experiences that can only be described as pastoral. At morning stand-to, facing east over no man's land, he saw 'marvellously beautiful dawns' accompanied by the morning-song of birds. He especially liked the moments when the sky was 'dark & the stars still out in the west & the dawn coming up in the east'. Once, he experienced this to perfection.[15] On the rare occasions later in life when he was awake at dawn, he would remember morning stand-to.

He noticed beauty where others did not. He saw it in 'improvisations, such as bits of sand-bag tied round people's legs' by which men acquired 'character & "picturesqueness"'. When his battalion occupied

75

*28. 'Harry Cook
1917 (Ypres sector?)'*

positions next to the French, he admired their revetments made of interwoven branches and saplings – wattling that reminded him of the weir at Rhos and stirred his fondness since childhood for all things interwoven. Even in the devastated landscape he saw a 'beauty of a strange sort that once experienced', he would later write, 'remains imprinted on the mind forever'.[16] He may be the only man on record to have thought no man's land beautiful, but then he was not prone to confusing aesthetics with other categories of evaluation.

More than anything else, he enjoyed the fellowship of his companions, whom he 'loved', some more than others. Friendship between soldiers, during this war especially, has been called homoerotic, and friendship between young men often is. Indication that his youthful charm stirred such feeling may be inferred from the words he heard 'more than once' from companions, 'I wish I knew your sister' – a wish equally suggestive, however, of heterosexual feeling. He later echoed the remark in his poetry (*SL* 16).[17]

The more erotic a friendship, the more exclusive, and his closest friendships were not especially so. Since before coming to France, one of his best friends was a machine-gunner named Reggie Allen, from Abertillery, north-west of Newport. Another was Leslie Poulter (ch. 6, fig. 47), who was in the Signals section of the battalion. He was partly of Swiss descent, a month younger than Jones but looked

29. *'shrapnel burst, 1916 Givenchy, supports'*

years older. He had volunteered at the age of 17 in 1914, in time to fight at Mons. He was courageous without being aware of it and unfailingly amusing.[18] Another friend was Harry Cook (fig. 28), who was, like Poulter, a signaller. He was regularly promoted for courage, intelligence, and efficiency and demoted for drunkenness. Allen, Poulter, and Cook were, like Jones, middle-class and highly intelligent. They were close, mutual friends.

In dugouts and between fatigues, Jones mostly talked with his platoon-mates in small groups about many things: death, women, mothers-in-law, irksome relatives, the tyranny of officers, and systemic military inequity. About these, he would remember, they spoke knowledgeably, sometimes wisely. Sometimes they obscenely mocked what they most cared about: women and sexual love. About politicians, government, the causes of war, society at large, and the characteristics of foreign nations, 'they mouthed the / catch-words of the Press.' Usually these gab-sessions 'cast all fear away' so that 'mirth had elbow-room' (*IP* MS).

A society of fellow-sufferers, they were, to one another, the chief consolation of military life. Theirs was the intimate, open society of

30. 'St Vaast in 1916'

the slum. All volunteers, whatever their class and background, they were basically friendly, trustful, and, even while bitterly complaining, dedicated. Jones would write in his preface to *In Parenthesis* that 'the "Bugger! Bugger!" of a man detailed, had often about it the "Fiat! Fiat!" of the Saints' (p. xii). Because of their enthusiasm, generosity and good humour, they were, in one another's eyes, the best of men. In many cases, their affection for each other would not have survived civilian life, but here, in shared squalor and danger, it was intensely and generally felt. For Jones, fellowship was the principal redeeming aspect of military life.

It also may have kept him from succumbing to fear. He was 'bloody frightened' in the trenches but, like most, unwilling to display fear that would unnerve his mates or elicit their contempt. About feeling afraid, he thought himself 'average'. He later said, 'I was young for my age. [. . .] I disliked it greatly, but there was a curious kind of exhilaration' mixed with the fear. By contrast, his sergeant – a Cockney who had been a professional burglar before the war and would be the prototype for Sergeant Snell of *In Parenthesis* – was usually anxious and often terrified, sometimes to the point of violent nausea.[19]

31. *'Front Trench early spring 1916'*

The day after Christmas, the Grenadier Guards, their initiators, withdrew, and the battalion was relieved in the front line by verbose, jocular Irish Guards. Two days later, the battalion was transported eleven miles north-west to reserve billets in Merville, a town dominated by its hall-tower and shaped to the serpentine curves of the river Lys behind its main street. It was larger than most towns in the region, and, perhaps for that reason, Jones thought it 'uncomfortable'. He had disliked leaving Warne, Winnall Down, and Llandudno – he hated leaving any place once he got used to it – and now, even though he was 'pretty scared in them', he *'positively disliked* coming out of the trenches'. 'I'm pretty cracked about "partings"', he later wrote.[20] At Merville they rested and underwent further training from 28 December till 6 January.

From here he wrote home, reassuring his mother that the trenches were nothing like those before Sebastopol in which one of her uncles had stood, as he had told her, knee-deep in blood. These in Flanders were, Jones wrote, 'merely ankle-deep in muddy water in places'.[21] He did not tell her of places where water was thigh-high – the terrain of the Richebourg sector was, in fact, the worst on the western front. The best ground was barely above sea level, and the Germans had taken the higher ground. Near La Bassée the line was below sea level. There, after a dam burst, men in dugouts had actually drowned. Any digging almost immediately struck water. Men joked about the feasibility of using torpedoes here. The muddy water was so cold that it could make a single icy shell of boots, puttees and breeches. For now, most casualties – from frost-bite, rheumatism and trench-foot – were caused by water and the cold.

The battalion began five months of regular tours of duty in the Richebourg-Neuve Chapelle line and in the Givenchy sector. The tours consisted of four periods of four to seven days spent respectively in front-line trenches, support trenches, reserve trenches, and divisional reserve. In all trenches, men were killed or wounded. In fact, the favourite targets of long-range enemy artillery during this period were the support and reserve lines. And most fire was in-coming. (British artillery, even light-field artillery, was at this time strictly rationed to about four rounds a day, so that requests for artillery support often received the reply 'Sorry, we've already fired our quota for today.') In the reserve line, men usually lived in the cellars of ruined houses. From here they serviced the forward trenches by making one or more journeys daily or nightly carrying food, water, material, or munitions. Miles further back at divisional reserve they were safe, apart from occasional aerial bombing at night, but they were, he would remember, 'continually being disturbed' by warnings of bombing and obliged in daytime to endure tedious training, drill and fatigues.[22]

On 7 January 1916, the battalion marched from divisional reserve at Merville nine miles south to reserve trenches at Richebourg-Saint-Vaast, 'a ghastly place'.[23] They remained four days in these trenches, where much work could only be done under cover of darkness, so that, here especially, night brought little sleep. In these trenches, on 10 January, they experienced their first enemy barrage. Under heavy fire, they were ordered forward from dugouts in the reserve line and began trudging through a communication trench toward the front line to relieve the 16th Battalion. Then, owing to the heavy shelling, they went back.[24] There they waited in full gear in candle-lit darkness, listening with the sensitivity of aesthetes, although the bombardment was an appalling trial, which Jones would commemorate (referring to himself as '79 Jones'):

> You stand by in billets and complain, for more than an hour, trussed up and girded, but at tea-time counter-pointing violences give the thing a new twist, the plain cadence modu- lates ominously – breaks all remembered records – he cuts the painter properly – flames uncontrol over the whole subsector. This nasty type of flamboyance makes you light another cigarette from the stub-end of the one before – makes Fatty sing loudly of the Armentieres lady – makes '79 Jones, in his far corner, rearrange and arrange again a pattern of match ends.
>   Each variously averts his perceptions, masks the inward abysm . . . . (IP 108-9)

Four hours after it began, the shelling decreased, then stopped, leaving two men dead, five wounded, and the battalion headed forward again, occupying the front trench at 8.30 that evening.

From now until June, they moved between trenches from Givenchy in the south to Picantin in the north.

On night sentry-duty now, aware of his comrades huddled round a fire under the lee-side of the trench or, in the reserve line, under the broken wall of a building, Jones wryly repeated to himself a circular chant from his childhood:

> It was a dark and stormy night.
> The brigands sat round their camp fire.
> The Chief said to Antonio, 'Antonio, tell us a tale',
> And the tale ran thus:

'It was a dark & stormy night,
The brigands sat round their camp fire . . .'[25]

In later years, when the rhyme came to mind, he would associate it with memories of soldiers huddled together.* He also bolstered his 'timid spirit', as he called it, by reciting to himself the poems of *Lays of Ancient Rome* that he had memorised.[26]

One dark and stormy night, he was on sentry-duty in a trench at Richebourg-l'Avoué, a village utterly destroyed because the front line ran through it, when the brigade commander, General L. A. E. Price-Davies, appeared round the traverse of a fire-bay. He was carrying his wooden staff, 4 feet 6 inches long, which was the regulation height of the parapet above the fire-step. He determined that here it was an inch or so over regulation height and ordered Jones and others present to make the adjustment. In the rainy dark they disassembled revetments, removed sandbags, emptied a portion of their contents, and restacked them – Jones and his co-workers regarding the result as ridiculously disproportionate to the effort.[27]

Price-Davies was slim, handsome, obstinately fastidious, and spoke slowly and primly. Behind his back, his fellow officers called him 'Jane'. He wore a unique, completely waterproof outfit resembling a pair of overalls, which Jones thought 'jolly nice and eminently practical' for endlessly wet trench life. Punctilious in making his rounds, Price-Davies was 'imperturbable', ignoring rifle-fire, machine-gun-fire, shrapnel, and even heavy bombardment. Jones saw him several times fully exposing himself to fire in daylight in order to measure the level of sandbags. His fearlessness had won him the Victoria Cross and Distinguished Service Order in South Africa, but the men thought it stupid. On one occasion in a support trench, Jones watched him stand out in the open during a heavy barrage with his subordinate officers – they were unable to run for cover without him – carefully undoing a package and saying, 'I so hate to waste string, especially in wartime.'

* He would paraphrase it for the epigraph of *The Anathemata* (p. 44) and subsequently write, 'It's a wonder' the words of this rhyme 'didn't get into *In Parenthesis*.'

When he got it open, he complained, 'When will my aunt learn that what I like is chocolate, not chocolates.'[28] A special concern of his was the collection and burial of the tins that littered the trenches. Later, in the Ypres sector, he would have the battalion devote a week to collecting enough to fill over 600 sandbags – a futile enterprise since every falling shell unearthed more tins. Jones was once within earshot of him while a Welsh battalion passed through a communication trench towards the front line, singing as it passed the brooding, melancholy hymns they generally sang. Totally anglicised, Price-Davies asked a Welsh-speaking brigade officer, 'Why do they sing

32. '(?) Feb-March (?) 1916 Forward trench La Bassée area front line (grenade store)'

such sad songs that sound like hymns? It's bad for morale, very bad!' Jones was dismayed at his insensitivity to the beauty of the singing.[29]

Always cold, Jones spent much of his free time, when not huddled around a fire, hunting for wood dry enough to burn. On one of his expeditions, he found half a door in the ruins of a farm building and put it on his back to carry to his platoon-mates. As he walked, he bent further and further under the weight of the door. Crab-like, he proceeded until his limited, downward vision encompassed a pair of spotless boots; and the voice of Colonel Bell said, 'What are you doing with that door?' Jones replied, 'I'm going to make a fire with it, sir.' The Colonel said, 'We pay rent to the French.' (Land for trenches was leased.) 'I'm not saying your regiment isn't brave, but you've got a bad reputation for stealing.' (Jones caught the allusion: 'Taffy was a Welshman, Taffy was a Thief'.) 'Take it back where you got it.' He did, and after further scrounging discovered some sticks to burn. The next day the half-ruined building and its detached half-door were, in his words, 'blown to buggery'.[30]

Jones had not ceased drawing – he carried in his pack a 7 by 4 ½ inch sketchbook. On Salisbury Plain, he had drawn men sleeping in their greatcoats, using haversacks as pillows. Now he drew bivvy mates or other infantrymen in their soft service caps, alone or in groups: one of a soldier kneeling on a fire-step and looking through a periscope (fig. 25); another of a man in the La Bassée area sitting against a wall at a grenade store and smoking a pipe (fig. 32); another, done in March, of two men sitting by a petrol-tin fire, one of them cooking, the working parts of their rifles burlap-wrapped against mud (fig. 24). These and his other sketches made in the trenches he later judged to be 'without any sense of form' and displaying 'no imagination', being only 'feeble impressionistic "sketches" much as might appear in any popular illustrated paper', but they may well convey more truth about life in the trenches than the less immediately rendered, stylised, highly finished work of official war artists.[31]

His lieutenant saw his drawings, thought his talent might be useful, and ordered him to make maps of no man's land while on patrol at night. One of the maps he drew early this year in the La Bassée sector survives, though too faint to reproduce: a 3 by 6 inch sketch on notepaper in which he indicates 'Our Trench' and, beyond, 'Ruins', 'Crater', a German listening post, and a German sentry post .

Patrols went out almost nightly to examine the strength of the enemy and 'foster the offensive spirit'. With half a dozen others, he would scurry in the darkness out through the British wire, drop on his belly as he approached the enemy line, and creep forward – carefully since the muddy earth hid sharp metal splinters. Going on patrol took nerve. No man's land was littered with the foetid corpses of participants of raids and previous patrols. As the men approached the enemy line, any sound they made – in the wire, amid the tin-cans and garbage thrown forward from the trench – was potentially fatal. When a Very flare went up, they froze, knowing that the slightest movement would be seen. When he could, Jones crawled into a shell-hole and stayed there, but usually he had to move along with the others.[32] It was important not to lose direction – like one patrol that concluded its night's work by jumping with relief into the enemy trench.

One night he went on patrol with an officer and two other men, one of them a sergeant named Morgan. They crawled up to the enemy wire. Jones could see the sentry's *Stahlhelm* moving back and forth in the trench. Suddenly Morgan loudly kicked a tin. Because they were young, nervous and in mortal danger, they began to laugh, shaking with stifled hilarity, unable to stop. The muffled noise increased their danger, which increased their laughter and their desperation to suppress it. Minutes later the hysteria subsided and, Jones would remember, 'We crept back as fast as we bloody well could.'[33]

Whenever possible now he volunteered to go on patrol. A few hours in no man's land exempted you from fatigue duty for the rest of the night, and fatigues were especially difficult for him because he was not strong enough to carry heavy weight long distances. He regarded patrols as only slightly more dangerous and considerably more exciting. 'As for the danger', he later said, 'there was nothing to it really. You just went out on patrol for a few hours, occasionally collided with Germans, mostly avoided them, and then, in my case, you just came back and went to bed.'[34] Later, for a cousin, he imitated himself whining to his sergeant to be assigned to a patrol instead of fatigue duty: 'Been wiring all the fucking afternoon – & told off for rations at 6:30. Why can't no. 3 do rations? Went over last night' (i.e. back to the kitchen). 'All right Copper Head, all right', said the sergeant, 'It's rations or Mr Smith's patrol. What you bloody like.' (His sergeant called him 'Copper Head' because of the light tinge to his brown hair to distinguish him from the other Joneses in the platoon.)[35]

Early in 1916 he went out on patrol to examine the enemy's wire. As he remembered,

It was a small party, 4 men including myself, a sergeant & I think a corporal under the command of a Lieutenant Best, for whom I had a liking. He wore a beautiful British Warm & a light Khaki muffler & when we got to the German wire immediately before the glassis [sic] of the front trench where the ground was soggy with mud we had to lie down as low as possible, Best whispered to me (I chanced to be next him), 'Blast this wet mud, I simply loathe putting my chin into the stuff', and then with great deliberation he drew out from the left-hand cuff of his British Warm a silk handkerchief (purple as far as I could see) and spread it carefully & squarely over the mud & then put his chin & indeed half his face on the handkerchief.

Jones regarded this as 'a rather grand thing to do'.[36]

He admired and imitated the educated lieutenants of his battalion and, wishing to be like them, used their slang, speaking of 'chaps' and 'blokes' and the 'Boche' (not a term used by Cockney privates). Poulter and probably Allen did the same – it was, for them, an identification with what Jones, at the time, called 'the better classes' – though he also adopted aspects of Cockney diction. His feelings for junior officers were not, however, easy or entirely agreeable because they were authority figures, of superior rank, and, for him, the pressure to avoid blunders was a distraction and a constant barrier.[37]

On 8 February he and his battalion left the trenches for rest and further training. In reserve billets, they discarded their warm, stylish sheepskin jackets because, it had suddenly become evident, they encouraged a population explosion of body lice. Even without the jackets, lice were a torment, breeding in the seams of clothing and leaving red bite-marks over the entire body except the head. In the forward trenches, men spent much of their time between fatigues hunting lice and cracking them between fingernails. In reserve billets, they searched blankets for lice. Once every few weeks, at divisional baths in reserve, they underwent delousing, which brought relief for only a few days, until resilient eggs hatched and the biting and itching resumed, increasing in ferocity until the next bath and change of clothes.

33. 'Givenchy 1916, very big mine crater with dugouts D.J.'

At divisional reserve, reveille was at 6 a.m., roll-call at 7, followed by the cleaning of rifles, and, at 8, breakfast. The rest of the morning consisted of inspections of arms and quarters and of a long session of drill. During lunch the regimental band gave a concert, which did not improve Jones's appetite. (All music by military bands or bands of any sort aroused in him 'something near to loathing'.) The period after lunch until 4 p.m. was devoted to organised games, mostly football. Officers played cricket, along with enlisted men good at the game. The least athletic of men, Jones participated only when required to. He enjoyed, however, watching rugby football, the preferred sport of the Welsh battalions and, he thought, one of the great creative achievements of Wales. (In later life, he would follow the rugby scores and root for Wales.) His friend Poulter was one of the best on the battalion teams. After games, the men were free, except for those on guard-duty, and could go to the canteen, the YMCA, or the Red-Cross hut to buy with their ten francs pay postcards, razor-blades, cigarettes, and food.[38]

At one of these, sometime early in the war, he made a peculiar purchase. A platoon-mate had asked to borrow his toothbrush. Unable to refuse, he lent it and received it back again but was dismayed by the request and unwilling to brush his own teeth with it, so he bought another, carrying two for the remainder of the war, one to use, the other a loaner.

Because divisional reserve was beyond the range of heavy shells, civilians lived nearby, and a major source of delight was 'screaming Froggie brats' (*IP* MS). Sometimes, twice a week or so, there were organised entertainments – a divisional concert or boxing match. Battalions and brigades occasionally held impromptu concerts. These consisted of songs, recitals, and skits. Motion pictures were sometimes shown. (He was a Charlie Chaplin fan.) Lights-out was at 9.30.

In the evenings he mixed with friends and got to know men outside his unit in his favourite among the many estaminets. Here he and his companions talked, drank, and smoked – by now, he was smoking cigarettes.[39] In an estaminet he could buy a meal, though the choice was limited to a fried egg or omelette and chips – this sector was known as the 'Egg and Chip Front'. It may have been here that he developed his taste for the simple omelette he later often ordered in London restaurants.

He had acquired two anthologies of poetry printed on thin paper, *Palgrave's Golden Treasury* and *The Oxford Book of English Verse 1250–1900*. Leaving one of these with his pack at Quartermaster Stores when going into the trenches, he carried the other, which he read when he had spare time.[40]

He also carried in his knapsack a piece of oil cloth to sit on as a precaution against piles – this at the insistence of his mother, who subscribed to the belief that sitting on damp cold surfaces causes haemorrhoids, an affliction that ran in the family.[41]

On 17 February 1916, the battalion marched from reserve billets six miles east into support trenches at Givenchy. Four nights later, they took over the front line on a slight hill rising over a plain. Givenchy had an evil reputation. Shell-fire had made it the most desolate place he had yet seen. The men called it, simply, 'the craters'. Here the enemy front trench was very close, separated from the British front line by only 'a solid briary brake of red rusted entanglements of wire'. The

34. '(leather equipment)
Festubert? in Front line
trench 1916, chap cooking'

place was 'a tangle of trenches', 'comfortless and untidy . . . saturated
with damp and broken revetment wire'. There were dugouts in the
sides of craters (fig. 33), but men mostly sheltered in makeshift cubby-
holes scraped into the parados. Fires were forbidden day and night, a
rule regularly broken.[42] Huge cavities pocked the area but not from
artillery – despite the high water table here, there was much under-
mining and countermining. The explosion of a mine was especially
unnerving because, unlike the bursting of an artillery shell, no sound
preceded it. Over the coming weeks, furthermore, mortar-fire became
nearly constant. Because of the flooding, the mining and the mortars,
these trenches would be, for the next three months, the hardest part
of the line to hold anywhere on the western front, and casualties
were high.

35. 'Front-line Festubert 'The Islands' 1916'; [on reverse] 'The Grouse Butts sector near Festubert'

After four days here, they marched back through snow four miles along a canal tow-path into reserve at Gorre, arriving on 26 February. The contrast was extreme. The flat farmland of Gorre, with standing woods to the south and west, was miraculously peaceful, an oasis in the wasteland – never shelled, now or later, though within easy range of enemy heavy guns. In billets here, the incessant rumble of the front was faint enough to be eclipsed by quite ordinary nearer noises. The location of the front was indicated on the horizon by bright yellow observation balloons and little white anti-aircraft blossoms rising in the paths of insect-like aeroplanes. After three days at Gorre under instruction by the Lancashire Fusiliers, they returned to trenches at Givenchy. In this sector, they moved twelve times, working through their tour in constant rain, the heaviest rainfall in March for 35 years. Over the coming weeks, they occupied trenches at Givenchy, Hingette, Le Touret and Festubert.

At Festubert, a mile north of Givenchy, the water-line was so high that instead of trenches there were only isolated sandbag breastworks on the surface of the swampy ground, one of which he sketched (fig. 35). The 'Islands' or 'Grouse-Butts', as the men called them, could be reached only at night on duckboard tracks over open ground. The men called the place 'Festering Hubert'. A member of his battalion later described the 'eerie business' of reaching 'the Islands' by 'walking boldly above ground, across ditches, and through the remains of barbed wire, past long unburied corpses'. Jones was once making such an approach at Festubert, crossing a plank bridge over a muddy ditch, when, suddenly, he felt utterly terrified, certain that he was about to be killed. The danger of being in the open so close to the enemy might seem justification enough for such sharp fear, but it was, to him, unaccountable – an eruption into consciousness of terror often felt but habitually repressed.[43] He finished crossing the plank and made his way to the designated breastwork. Never, for the rest of the war, would he knowingly feel so afraid.

By the beginning of April, the battalion had participated in no raid or assault and had defended against none, yet casualties were commonplace. There were walking cases, stretcher cases, and ground-sheet cases, the latter sometimes requiring a reassembling of body-parts. Owing mostly to artillery and trench-mortar fire, in four months they had lost 105 men, more than 20 per cent of the battalion – 25 killed, 80 wounded. Five days at Givenchy in April cost them five killed and nineteen wounded.

On 13 April the battalion received steel helmets. Synonymous with later cultural memory of the war, the new 'tin hats' resembled those worn by medieval foot-soldiers and completed Jones's sense of affinity with medieval infantrymen, an affinity already visually established by the Short Sword Bayonet (fig. 36). When not fixed to the rifle, this 18-inch blade hung from the belt in its scabbard reaching to the knee. This feeling of affinity with fighting men of an earlier age was widely shared. Propaganda posters regularly depicted knights in armour, and many thought of the war in relation to chivalry, the standard by which military conduct was still measured even by those who found it wanting. Ernst Jünger thought 'chivalry' survived until July 1916. Crown Prince Rupprecht of Bavaria considered the poison gas that he helped to develop 'unchivalrous'.[44]

36. Sword Bayonet, 'Front-line 1916—why not fixed bayonette?'

Throughout the war, Jones and most infantrymen he knew felt this continuity with the past. It was officially encouraged by battalion lectures and by the ritual incantation of the battle honours of the 23rd Foot at the beginning of official pronouncements. Recalling battles since the late seventeenth century, these were potent names:

> Namur, Blenheim, Ramillies, Oudenarde, Malplaquct, Dettingen, Minden, Corunna, Martinique, Albuera, Salamanca, Badajoz, Vittoria, Pyrenees, Nivelle, Orthez, Toulouse, Peninsula, Waterloo, Alma, Inkerman, Sevastopol, Lucknow, Ashantee, Burma, Ladysmith, Peking.

Feelings of continuity with the past were romantic, especially early on, but would survive, with diminishing idealism, in the more mechanised and deadly later years of the war. It was not merely a product of propaganda, nor had it now much to do with merely being in the army. He 'felt it only when actually living the life of the Forward Area, in the actual trenches or their immediate vicinity'. There, he would remember, 'a strange metamorphosis seemed to take place in one's feelings', a change to 'a feeling of reality, gravity, urgency. It was there that one felt in communion with all the past.' The feeling was never, for him, merely a matter of external, physical resemblances. He repeatedly thought, 'Ah well, this is what chaps must have felt like during recent or remote historical combat.' In his war epic, he would allude to battles of the historical and legendary past, '*not*', he writes, 'because I *consciously* wished or attempted to restore those far-past heroic struggles, but because, in my experience, men behaved in much the same way as those past heroes had behaved'. In the trenches, he became convinced that any distinction between past and present was superficial, accidental, largely unreal. History had not ended; it continued. In 1960 he would approvingly check in the margin of a Sorbonne dissertation on his writing the assertion that during the war 'he had for the first time been made aware of living history'.[45]

From Givenchy they went to Gorre for three days rest, then

37. Tin Hats. 'N.W. of Ypres (probably Elverdinghe)'

endured three days of purposeless, circular marching that gave unusual validity to a daily complaint by a long-faced Cockney in his platoon, 'If it ain't him over there, it's those beauties back at H.Q. seem to 'ave it in for our mob'.[46] Then they took over the front at Moated Grange and Laventie. On 24 April they moved into reserve at La Gorgue for a week of further training, which, as always, Jones hated. On 1 May, in pouring rain, he was in the line at Picantin, where trenches were so sodden that rotten sandbags burst and trench walls tended to collapse. After being wet through for four days in a soup of grey mud, they moved on 5 May into the front line at Fauquissart.

Here, on the 7th, they carried out their first raid. Jones volunteered but only the big and strong were chosen, since hand-to-hand combat was anticipated. So he was assigned, instead, to the covering party and at 11.30 slipped into no man's land with the raiders in order to fire on the flanking sections of the enemy line. As on other such occasions, someone commented, 'Bloody dark, mate', and was answered, 'Christ, mate, it's a gift.' (Years later Jones would recall this remark with delight when he discovered the darkness of night called a gift in Book VIII of the *Aeneid*.) Advancing silently through no man's land, the raiders came upon a German wiring party finishing its work and followed it into their trench. There they attacked, hurling over 200 grenades and killing most of the enemy, unarmed and crowded together, struggling frantically to get grenades out of a store. The raiders waded into the carnage with bludgeons and revolvers. They withdrew at 2.30 a.m., Jones's party covering their rear, and were swept by machine-gun fire that killed the young officers leading the raiding party.[47] When he scurried back into the trench, Jones saw the few prisoners taken in the raid literally shaking with fear. His sergeant-major, who had not been involved in the action, grabbed one of them, twisted his arm up behind his back and began frog-marching him down the trench. Jones and his companions protested, 'You can't do that, sir' and stopped him. (Sergeant-majors, he later said, 'were almost all bastards'.)[48]

There were other instances of indignation at mistreating prisoners – something he and his mates would not tolerate. Later he wrote about the killing of men:

> I don't recall that we felt anything like the shock & distress felt by many at home in contemplating the wastage of life, etc. etc . . . we took much of this for granted – rather as though it were part of some unavoidable natural calamity – or a *bit* like that. Yet the ill-treatment of a prisoner could still be repellent to us – that would by no means be taken as a necessary part of the state of affairs . . . though there were indeed, as always, bastards who if no one was looking, would act against this code, and circumstances when a number of persons might do so together.

Despite propaganda, he and most of his comrades did not hate the German infantryman, who, they felt, shared their suffering, but felt toward him 'a detachment which inhibits moral judgement of others, more especially those upon whom we are called to inflict wounds'.[49]

General headquarters would consider the raid the most successful carried out in the division and the third best so far by the British army.[50] Well over 50 Germans were killed or wounded. British casualties were light: two dead, eleven wounded, one missing. What most impressed Jones, however, was the testimony of the raiders that the sides and bottom of the German trenches were completely lined with wood and entirely dry.

The next day, he looked at the British dead on the enemy barbed wire – 'you could see them plainly, hung like rag-merchants' stock, when the light was favourable' (*IP* 106). One of these was a lieutenant he had especially liked, 'an attractive man, very absent minded, and also fair-haired', reminiscent of the bare-headed squire in Paolo Uccello's *The Rout of San Romano* in the National Gallery. (He would commemorate this lieutenant twice in *In Parenthesis*, as Mr Rhys and as Mr Jenkins who mourns Mr Rhys.)[51]

The army was running out of front-line junior officers. Their casualty rate was high because their Sam Browne belts, close-cut coats, and riding breeches gave them a distinctive silhouette, making clear targets for enemy sharp-shooters. Senior officers were told to search the ranks for men who might be promoted. Because Jones's accent was middle-class, Colonel Bell sent for him and asked why he was not commissioned. Jones replied that he was not 'that sort of person'. Bell said, 'That's nonsense, you know', and Jones continued, 'I am totally incompetent, sir.' Pressed to explain, he said that he was incapable of ordering people about. (He thought, but did not say, that he would not mind being a general.) Although he admired the cultured manners of junior officers, he disliked the officer-class because most were arrogant and deficient in the humour which helped make present conditions endurable and which his fellow privates had abundantly. The only advantage he could see to being a junior officer was the right to wear a lioness-coloured British warm. Bell persisted, 'Look here, Jones, you're shirking your duty. As an educated man, you should put in for a commission – by the way, what is your school?' Jones replied, 'Camberwell School of Arts and Crafts.' 'Oh', said Bell with a change of expression. He dropped the subject and terminated the interview. Never again was Jones asked to accept a commission.[52]

At another time, he was offered the chance to be a batman, an officer's personal servant. Batmen had an easy life because they escaped fatigues on the pretext of prior obligations and, when moving, loaded their equipment on wagons with that of their officers. Jones declined this opportunity also because he preferred privates to officers and wished to stay with his friends.[53]

Through the rest of May, they moved between support trenches and the front line near Fauquissart. Here they were heavily shelled twice a week on average and suffered one casualty every two days. They contributed to a British barrage by firing rifle-grenades into the enemy forward trench for three hours. From here they moved into divisional reserve at La Gorgue, then into the front line before Moated Grange, and from there into support trenches at Riez Bailleul.

The warm weather brought with it mosquitoes and, especially, flies. Attracted by latrines and corpses, flies swarmed above and in the trenches, shrouding any exposed food. Men sprayed creosote to discourage them, which added tang to the composite stench of the forward areas, a smell that strengthened as the weather warmed.

Despite policy forbidding diaries, Jones kept a tiny pocket diary in which he entered, for 29 May, 'Blankets taken in – rotten to find none when we came back from the trenches.' This entry is one of only three to survive. The following year in the Ypres sector, he would leave his diary with his pack in a dugout and return, hours later, to find dugout, pack and diary blown to bits by a direct hit.

On 2 June the battalion returned to the familiar Richebourg sector, and made for the front-line trench near Moated Grange. While they moved along a communication trench towards the line, someone coming from the rear announced that Kitchener had been drowned at sea. Jones was passing a wet and weary Cockney who paused in his work to say, 'Oh, 'e 'as, 'as 'e. Well roll on fuckin Duration.'[54] To these men, no man's death was important news.

Having experienced six months of combat, Jones was now a seasoned infantryman, expert at survival. Though clumsy at drill – 'grotesquely incompetent, a knocker-over of piles, a parade's despair' (IP xv) – he was nevertheless an efficient soldier. Late in life, when a friend jokingly accused him of having been an incompetent soldier, he was so indignant that when they met again a week later, he asked him to justify the accusation.[55] The battalion as a whole was now considered expert at trench-warfare, and, in the front line here, they were entrusted for the first time with the instruction of a unit new to the front.

On the night of 7 June at 1 a.m., he took part in a patrol to inspect a mine crater. A lieutenant in the forward trench at the time recalls:

> one of our subalterns took out a patrol to scour the slopes of the crater to make sure that the enemy had not secured a hiding place on its eastern face. . . . Soon we heard a bomb bursting . . . then many more in quick succession: the enemy [in trenches] did not fire, neither did we, lest the wrong men be hit. All was darkness . . . the flashes showed that the tussle was pitched near the crater, but after a dozen bombs were thrown, silence came again.[56]

The British patrol had met an enemy patrol. In his diary for the day, Jones recorded, 'Went on patrol with Lieut. Frost in search of working party on German crater. Bombs thrown. Frost – splendid, but a bit "wild".' Despite the exchange of grenades and the patrol's lingering in no man's land for an hour after the encounter (which infuriated at least one superior officer), no one was hurt.

Courage of the sort that made Lt. Frost 'splendid' meant a lot to Jones. Two weeks before, a lieutenant in the battalion had received the Albert Medal for groping in the mud to retrieve a submerged live grenade and tossing it away in time to save several lives. There were many acts of heroism, some honoured, many not. Without ever laying claim to courage himself, Jones admired it above all other virtues. War demanded it to an extreme degree, but he later saw no essential difference between 'what we call war and peace' in this respect. 'That's why', he would say, 'fortitude is *the* cardinal virtue because without fortitude, which is the same thing as courage, you can't have charity, you can't do anything because you're too cowardly – you're unjust because you're too cowardly.'[57]

For 8 June, he writes in his diary, 'Big bombardment on the right at 'stand-to' bombing attack by Bantams – glad to get relieved by the 16th RWF.' During their six days in this subsector, the battalion lost six men, two killed, four wounded.

In reserve, warm weather intensified enjoyment of fields high with grass and poppy blossoms, flittered over by white and yellow butterflies. Absence of tension and fresh memory of the grey monochrome and stench of the forward zone allowed him to appreciate this sweet-smelling, richly coloured aspect of nature as never before. The men lounged bareheaded in the sunshine, reading newspapers, playing cards, smoking, feeling on their faces the warm spring breezes.

Nearly from the beginning, the estaminets in reserve had been as filled with rumours as with tobacco smoke. Shortly after the men first arrived at the front, they heard of a mutiny in a French battalion that had been dealt with sternly. There were rumours of decimation – the execution of one in ten – which were dismissed as 'damned nonsense'. (Only late in life would he learn that rumour had been true: an entire French division had mutinied and been decimated.) At one time, it was rumoured that they were going to the Macedonian front and would be issued pith helmets. Always there was a rumour of the coming 'Great Push' that would see the triumph of Britain, France, and Russia over Germany. About this they were confident, even enthusiastic. They thought this might be an offensive newly rumoured to take place to the south 'in conjunction with the Frogs'.[58] That offensive, originally expected in the spring, was now to take place this summer. It would be the Battle of the Somme.

NOTES TO CHAPTER 3

1 Colin Hughes, p. 9; to René Hague, 9–15 July 1973; *IP* MS.

2 To René Hague, June 1967; DJ in conversation with author, 24 August 1972; to David Blamires, 6 November 1966; to Harman Grisewood, 1 February 1971; to Sir John Cecil-Williams, unposted, 22 December 1951.

3 For many details in this and the subsequent chapter I rely on Llywelyn Wyn Griffith, *Up to Mametz* (London: Faber and Faber, 1931). Griffith was a member of C Company in DJ's battalion. He records the dogfight (p. 17); *IP* MS.

4 DJ in conversation with author, 31 August 1972.

5   To Colin Wilcockson, 19 December 1956.

6   Stanley Honeyman, interviewed June 1991; to Sister Mary Ursula, draft n.d.; to René Hague, 6 July 1970; DJ to Edward Hodgkin, interviewed 5 August 1987.

7   To Aneirin Talfan Davies, 13 March 1956.

8   DJ interviewed by Jon Silkin, 1971; DJ interviewed by Peter Orr, early 1970s.

9   To Harman Grisewood, 25 December 1930; A 216.

10   To Harman Grisewood, 16 May 1940; DJ interviewed by Peter Orr, early 1970s.

11   *IP* MS; letter frag. n.d., [1950].

12   DJ in conversation with author; DJ to Blissett, pp. 107, 120; DJ did not mention the words of the Maconachie advertisement.

13   DJ, 'Somewhere in France' May 1917, typescript.

14   *IP* MS; Bernard Wall to Tony Stoneburner, 5 May 1966.

15   To Helen Sutherland, 9 February 1948.

16   To Peter Levi, 29 October 1963.

17   *IP* MS; to Saunders Lewis, 6 May 1961.

18   DJ to Blissett, pp. 133, 81; to Tony Stoneburner, 30 July 1969.

19   DJ interviewed by Peter Orr, early 1970s; quoted in Angela Gloria Donati Dorenkamp, '*In the Order of Signs*', An Introduction to the Poetry of David Jones (Ph.D. diss., Univ of Connecticut, 1974), p. 19; *IP* 42; Anthony Bailley, 'The Front Line', typescript, February 1973; DJ in conversation with author, 31 August 1972.

20   *IP* 116; to Janet Stone, 13 October 1959.

21   To Bernard Bergonzi, 11 November 1965.

22   To Mr Korda, 16 February 1962; to Tom Burns, 4 September 1940.

23   To René Hague, 9–15 July 1973.

24   DJ to Blissett, p. 74.

25   DJ recited this for Tony Stoneburner, who recorded it in his notes, 20 October 1964.

26   To Tony Stoneburner, 20 December 1964 draft, unposted n.d. [December 1964]; to Harman Grisewood, 9 October 1971.

27   To René Hague, 9–15 July 1973; to Colin Hughes, draft n.d.

28   To René Hague, 9–15 July 1973; to Colin Hughes, draft n.d.

29   To Harman Grisewood, 9 October 1971.

30   DJ in conversation with author, 24 August 1972.

31   DJ, 'Life for Jim Ede' (5 September 1935), second correction of typescript, 3 May 1943. See also DJ to Blissett, p. 23; Adam Thorpe, 'Distressed Perspectives', *Poetry Review* 86 (Spring 1996), p. 56.

32   DJ in conversation with author, 9 September 1972.

33   DJ to Blissett, p. 95; DJ, quoted in 'David Jones – Maker of Signs' (BBC, British Council), script broadcast on Radio 3, 6 November 1975, incorporating interviews by Peter Orr and Jon Silkin.

34   DJ quoted in 'David Jones – Maker of Signs'.

35   DJ interviewed by Jon Silkin, 1971; to René Hague, 3 June 1935; Maurice Bradshaw interviewed by Tony Stoneburner, 1975.

36   To Harman Grisewood, 12 January 1974.

37 DJ interviewed by Peter Orr, early 1970s; DJ, 'Somewhere in France' May 1917, typescript.
38 MS draft n.d. [c. 1965]; Stanley Honeyman, interviewed 21 June 1986; MS draft n.d. [c. 1965]; DJ interviewed by Jon Silkin, 1971; Arthur Giardelli interviewed, 8 June 1986; DJ quoted in 'From David Jones's Locker', *Manchester Guardian*, 11 February 1972.
39 DJ to Petra Tegetmeier, interviewed 3 October 1987.
40 DJ in conversation with author, 1 August 1972; DJ, 'For the Front', *Tablet* (13 January 1940); Blissett heard him say that he carried only 'one book', p. 107.
41 Stanley Honeyman interviewed, 9 October 1987.
42 Munby, p. 16; to René Hague, 9-15 July 1973; *IP* 186; DJ interviewed by Peter Orr, summer 1972.
43 Griffith, p. 63; DJ to Blissett, p. 122.
44 DJ interviewed by Peter Orr, early 1970s; Modris Eksteins, *Rites of Spring: The Great War and the Birth of the Modern Age* (New York: Doubleday), p. 162.
45 To Peter Levi, 29 October 1963; to John H Johnston, 23 March 1962, 30 September 1963, 16 May 1962; Catherine Ivanier's thesis on *The Anathemata* (Paris: Sorbonne, 1960), preface.
46 To Harman Grisewood, 25 August 1967.
47 Hughes, p. 170.
48 Annotations to Munby, p. 16; to Jackson Knight, 28 April 1959; DJ interviewed by Jon Silkin, 1971; conversation with author, 4 June 1971.
49 To Harman Grisewood, Laetare Sunday 1957; MS draft n.d.; to *The Times*, 14 December 1960; 'A Soldier's Memories', p. 506.
50 Munby, p. 16.
51 Hughes, p. 12.
52 Sarah and Maurice Balme, interviewed 24 June 1988; to Dorothea Travis, 18 March 1974; DJ interviewed by Peter Orr, early 1970s; DJ to Blissett, p. 78; DJ interviewed by Jon Silkin, 1971.
53 DJ to Blissett, p. 77.
54 To Harman Grisewood, 18 February 1960.
55 The friend was Peter Orr, interviewed 2 June 1986.
56 Griffith, p. 149.
57 DJ interviewed by Jon Silkin, 1971.
58 To Harman Grisewood, 24 February 1963; DJ, 'Somewhere in France' May 1917, typescript; DJ interviewed by Jon Silkin, 1971; *IP* 103.

CHAPTER 4

THE SOMME

On 10 June, in the Neuve Chapelle line, the Division received orders to begin marching south. On the morning of the 11th, they gathered by the Lys River and marched away from the familiar places of the Richebourg front. Each private carried his full pack and equipment, weighing, because it was summer, only 60 pounds. (Helmet and boots weighed an additional seven pounds.) Since it wasn't raining, the divisional band, marching ahead, played to give rhythm to the marching. In the sweltering June heat, they needed the encouragement, though it may not have extended to Jones, owing to his hatred of bands.

After cramped life in water-logged trenches, consecutive days of rapid marching under full packs blistered the feet of large numbers of men. More were crippled than went to the medical officer though, since no one liked joining the 'cripples squad', which, Jones later wrote, was 'an altogether depressing, ignominious, exhausting affair to be involved in'. The officially crippled were paraded hours earlier than the rest and allowed to march more slowly. '"For Christ's sake don't fall out" was the best neighbourly advice to anyone inclined to faint by the way.' Not that Jones's feet blistered. His mother had sent him soft woollen socks, which he wore under the hard grey army issue that had to be visible to inspecting officers. Throughout the war, his parents sent him a new pair of soft wool socks every few weeks. He would never have blisters nor, he said, did he mind marching.[1]

Most mornings, reveille was at 3.30 so that they could cover as much ground as possible before the noon heat. Company billets were often far from battalion assembly points. Traffic on crossroads caused miles-long traffic jams and hours of waiting. Once they waited while a French division passed – singing, big-hipped Burgundians who marched out of step, scandalising the British. Jones noticed, however, 'a rhythmic movement in those mob-like companies' and felt 'for the first time' that he was seeing 'something . . . of the dense columns of the Armies of the Revolution'. Earlier, before beginning the long march south, he had been 'amazed' to see a troop of French cavalry in steel breast-plates and helmets with horsetail plumes – the metal parts covered with khaki but otherwise looking as if 'on the road to Moscow or Waterloo'.[2]

Leaving the flatness of Flanders, the battalion entered the wooded hills of Artois. On the 14th they reached Floringhem, where they spent the night. It was good to be above ground and out of the mud. As feet eventually healed, spirits lifted, and they sang as they marched. On the 15th, they came to Bailleul-aux-Cornailles. So far, they had marched 35 miles.

Nearby at St Pol, they began ten days training in large-scale man-oeuvres and trench-assault, combined with mindless drill meant to reduce them to automatons. The general staff doubted whether these enlisted men would otherwise retain discipline during a frontal assault on strongly fortified enemy positions. Commanding the main attacking formation of the Fourth Army was General Henry Rawlinson. To ensure discipline, he had decided to conduct the assault at a leisurely walk in strict formation with rifles at the high port position (diagonally before the chest). The men were forbidden to run or break into short dashes between cover, which was the usual and much safer manner of assault, until 20 yards from the enemy trench. As a consequence of this original tactic, Rawlinson would be responsible for far more British casualties in this battle than any German general. He would also neglect to coordinate artillery fire on German batteries, leaving the matter wholly to the initiative of individual corps commanders, none of whom had commanded heavy artillery during battle. As a result, German artillery would take an appalling toll on the infantry.

High-ranking British officers had been trained to refight the battle of Waterloo. They believed that morale determined the outcome of battle and that, as in earlier wars, the attacker had the psychological advantage. In fact, however, the machine-gun, the modern rifle, barbed wire and artillery now gave enormous advantage to the defender.

On 26 June, as part of a larger movement in which the 38th Division joined the Second Army Corps, the battalion commenced marching the remaining 45 miles to the Somme. They travelled in a wide arc behind the lines, moving to Vacquerie-le-Boucq near Rubempré. Here, Jones and his companions, seeing Indian cavalry massed in preparation for battle, laughed aloud.[3] The cavalry, they knew – as the General Staff apparently didn't – would take no part in fighting.

On the 27th they moved to Bernaville and rested for two days. The men bathed and swam and strolled, mingling freely, joking and gossiping. At one end of the village, Jones watched a French priest strolling in his presbytery garden, reciting his breviary among bean plants pollinated by bees while artillery droned, bee-like, in the distance – an experience of antithetical symbolism that he would incorporate in his war epic (*IP* 117–8).

On the 30th they covered the greatest distance so far in a single day, 18 miles, and entered the rolling chalk land of the Somme. Exhausted, they arrived at midnight at Puchevillers where they waited in reserve throughout 1 July.[4] On this day the battle began. The British Fourth Army attacked the Germans along the front north of the Somme river and were checked on the centre and left. On the 2nd, Colonel Bell read a rescript from General Headquarters claiming success in the previous day's assault. The announcement concluded with permission to cheer, and they cheered. Years later 'gnawing thoughts' would well up in Jones at this memory. That day's 'success' incurred 57,470 British casualties, among them his art-school friend Harold Hawkins, who was terribly mangled and crippled for life.[5] It would be remembered as the bloodiest day in British military history.* One of the few actual British successes of the day was in the south, the capture of Mametz village.

In the evening, every man carrying the extra weight of an addi-

---

* Of these casualties, 21,000 were killed or mortally wounded. This was not, as is often claimed, the greatest loss of life in battle on a single day: the French had lost 27,000 on 14 August 1914.

tional 100 rounds of ammunition in two bandoliers round his neck, they moved north six miles to Lealvillers. They remained there until 7 p.m. in the evening on the 3rd, then marched eight miles to Ribemont-sur-Ancre, arriving at 2 a.m. on 4 July. Continually now they heard, and were mightily impressed by, the roar of the British barrage, which was on a scale far surpassing any bombardment in previous warfare.

Several times while on the move, Jones saw stacked rows of freshly made coffins – even though casualties were customarily buried without them. Like the poet Charles Wolfe (in the anthology he carried), he considered coffins 'useless'.[6] Nor were they particularly ominous – everyone knew that deaths would far exceed availability of wooden boxes.

General Rawlinson had wanted to attack the pushed-back German line frontally uphill between Mametz Wood and Trones Wood to the east, but his superior, Douglas Haig, insisted on first capturing Mametz Wood to secure the left flank of the main attacking force, and Rawlinson, though unconvinced, agreed to do what he was told.[7]

From Ribemont the battalion marched two miles south to Treux, joining up with the 15th Corps, and then eight miles to the shattered village of Mametz. At noon on the 5th they moved east through its red and grey ruins and at 8 p.m., occupied forward trenches in preparation for an assault on the wood, north-east of the village. In these trenches throughout the 6th and 7th, they endured continuous, systematic bombardment by enemy 5.9 howitzers. Casualties for the battalion were high – 58 killed and wounded, including victims of shell-shock.

On the 7th at 6.30 in the evening, what the battalion diary calls a 'small operation' (not involving Jones) commenced against the southern portion of the wood but was immediately terminated because of daunting strength of enemy machine-gun fire. The aborted attempt cost them twelve casualties – a small contribution to the 10,000 per day the British were now losing along this front.

At 2.30 a.m. on the 8th, Jones's battalion was relieved and went into brigade reserve at Minden Post in a place the men called 'Happy

38. 'Bivouacking in Happy Valley before attack on Mametz Wood'

Valley' (fig. 38). Here they bivouacked in the open for the day and rested. On a grassy knoll, Jones joined Reggie Allen and Leslie Poulter, reclining, nonchalantly watching the occasional enemy heavy shell shatter one of the distant rows of tents. They talked about the coming assault and about conscientious objectors – Allen objecting bitterly to the pacifism of 'Mr Bertrand-bloody-Russell' and dead-pan Poulter announcing to imaginary Caesars, 'We who are about to die salute you.' Speaking very little, Jones mostly listened to the comical exchange between informed, passionate Allen and equally informed, outrageous Poulter. They spoke of H. G. Wells's new book, of Rupert Brooke's death, of the Greek Venizelos, who Allen said was important, 'of the losses of the battalion since they came out, of the stupidity of the New Q.M., of the discomfort of having no greatcoats, . . . of the neutrality of Spain'. About the British barrage roaring in the background, Poulter was sceptical, saying, 'The fire power is there all right, but have we concentrated on the right targets?'[8] (As we have seen, he was right to be sceptical.) Before long they returned to their units to spend the night on the open field, catching what sleep they could amid the shriek-and-crash of incoming shells.

39. *The Centre of Mametz Village, roller on left,* Illustrated London News, 22 July 1916

At noon on the 9th the battalion moved forward to take part in a general attack on Mametz Wood by the entire 38th Division. They passed a cemetery on their right where artillery had caused gruesome general upheaval. Marching again between the smashed houses of Mametz, Jones noticed again (as he had four days before) in wreckage close to the road a large, heavy metal roller incongruously undamaged (fig. 39). Beyond the village they entered Fritz and Dantzig trenches and awaited the order to attack. For two hours they waited, their emotions alternating between fear and desire – desire to be elsewhere or (as in the days immediately preceding) that what was about to happen would not come to pass – the time punctuated, for Jones, by vivid perception of minute particulars that affirmed his physical existence on his patch of chalky dirt. At 2.30 in the afternoon, word was passed along that the assault was cancelled. The reason, which they did not know, was their division had to wait for the replacement of its commander, Major-General Ivor Philipps. He and another divisional commander were being replaced for a failed assault on the wood three days earlier, which had cost the division four battalions. Neither of the sacked divisional commanders had authored the catastrophic plan of attack, but Rawlinson and Haig required scapegoats.[9] For Jones and his battalion-mates, the two hours in the assault trench had been like a mock execution. Physically and emotionally drained, they marched all night back into Minden Post, arriving at 6.30 in the morning.

This marching up and back and up and back again carrying 85 pounds (full pack and ammunition) with almost no sleep left the men exhausted and demoralised. After midnight, on 10 June, Captain Thomas Elias brought orders once more to attack Mametz Wood.* In the dark, they marched a third time through the village, to take up reserve positions behind the 14th and 16th Battalions.[10]

The wood was (and remains today) a thick forest, a mile deep and roughly three-quarters of a mile wide, about 220 acres, much of it clogged by dense underbrush. It had been a hunting park and was the largest wood in the Somme battlefield (figs. 40, 41).[11] Two east-west rides crossed the breadth of the wood, intersected by a central north-south ride to form a lopsided Greek double cross. On a map, the wood is shaped like the state of Texas with the British line to the south running roughly along the 22nd parallel. The wood was held by experienced troops: the Lehr regiment of the Prussian 3rd Guards at the front and, behind them, units of the 16th Bavarian and the 122nd Württemberg regiments.[12] They were supplied and reinforced from a second line, 300 yards north of the northern edge of the wood. The flanks of the wood were strongly defended by German machine-gun emplacements. The British High Command considered it so nearly impregnable that it had been omitted as an objective in the initial attack of 1 July. Of the 2,000 men who had attacked it on the 6th, not one had reached it. Now the 15th Battalion, along with the other three battalions in the 113rd Brigade, was to attack the portion of the wood west of the central ride at a walking pace without flanking support over unpromising ground in the face of machine-gun and artillery fire. It was to be a simple frontal assault with no attempt to outflank the

---

* Years later, Jones would be startled when rereading Malory to find that 'Captain Elias came on the morn' to do battle (X, 29).

40. Distant view of 'Mametz Wood before the attack'

wood and depending for success solely on a three-to-one superiority in numbers.[13]

Having repeatedly marched back and forth in the previous days and having slept little the night before, they were, as Jones later put it, 'in a somewhat pathetic state'. (Later a rumour would circulate among the troops that the divisional commander was severely reprimanded for bringing exhausted troops into action.) At 2.15 a.m., they moved into Bunny Trench, just north of Mametz village. Then, at 3.30 a.m., a heavy British bombardment fell on the forward edge of the wood, swallowing all other sound. A smoke barrage was laid down along the western and eastern approaches to the wood, drawing some fire to those areas, where the enemy thought screened infantry were advancing. At 4.15, the 14th and 16th Battalions attacked up the open middle in clear view of the enemy. While the first waves advanced, Jones and his battalion moved with bayonets fixed and in attack formation from Bunny Trench 500 yards forward and to the right into Queens Nullah (fig. 41) on high ground immediately fronting the wood. (The nullah was a long ditch deeper than an ordinary trench – 'nullah' is Indian Army for gully.) As he moved up, Jones saw waves of men from the other battalions slowly advancing towards the wood. To him, it was 'an impressive sight'.[14] Flanking enemy machine-gun fire pouring in from emplacements beyond the western flank – from Wood Trench, Wood Support Trench, and Acid Drop Copse (fig. 41) – thinned considerably the impressive waves of slowly walking men. Enemy artillery also took a terrible toll. It was the most frightfully intense artillery fire they had been subjected to. Shells burst just above and in the nullah. Casualties mounted. Noise was sometimes deafening, the air thick with smoke and chalk-dust.

Jones and his companions hugged the earth. Nearby, his colonel casually stood, unnecessarily exposed. Emerging immaculately from the smoke and dust, another officer called out to him, 'Well, Bell!' – a rhyme that would be preserved in *In Parenthesis* (154) – and they proceeded to reminisce about their service together in India. Jones was prevented from hearing more of the conversation by agonised screaming of a badly wounded man beside him but he admired the composure of the officers and their indifference to danger and to the probable imminent killing or maiming of Bell, who was to lead the charge.[15]

As the men awaited the order to attack, the 16th Battalion was twice beaten back, and then its survivors regrouped in the nullah to join in the attack by Jones's battalion. The men of A Company went over first. In B Company, the four platoons formed into long lines to proceed separated by a distance of 100 yards. As they waited, machine-gun fire striking the lip of the nullah dusted them in chalk powder. A man beside Jones yelled in his ear, 'Two minutes to go', and he passed it on. As anxiety reached its peak, he noticed, on the white earth beneath his face, insects indifferent to the war and to his fear. Briefly in the smothering sound of gunfire, he heard on his right one of the most moving things he would ever hear, the 14th Battalion singing in Welsh 'Jesu lover of my soul'.[16] Faintly, over unmodulated thundering drum-fire, he heard a shrill whistle and saw the lieutenant of his platoon, R. G. Rees, wave them forward. Along with the others in his company, he clambered up the chalky slope and over the top, fear vanishing in activity and confusion.

Almost immediately, Lieutenant Rees, walking just ahead of him, was shot dead. Jones would recreate his fall in poetic slow motion in *In Parenthesis*:

> He sinks on one knee
> and now on the other,
> his upper body tilts in rigid inclination
> this way and back;
> weighted lanyard runs out to full tether,
> swings like a pendulum
> and the clock run down.
> Lurched over, jerked iron saucer over tilted brow,
> clampt unkindly over lip and chin
> nor no ventaille to this darkening
> and masked face lifts to grope the air
> and so disconsolate;
> enfeebled fingering at a paltry-strap –
> buckle holds,
> holds him blind against the morning. (166)[17]

No man's land was 500 yards of wild, uncropped grass, thistles, wild flowers, and self-sown mustard and wheat. Like a mechanism perversely preset to move slowly, they walked across 60 yards of plateau, scurried down a steep 30 to 50 foot incline, and slowly walked up the bare, gradually rising slope towards high ground where the enemy waited, firing at them. The walk took four minutes, a passage through a maelstrom of rifle and machine-gun bullets, shrapnel and shell-casing fragments flying at every angle – a thousand potential deaths and maimings with no protecting cover. The noise was beyond hearing, the quaking earth erupting, the air thick with smoke, chalky dirt, steel, bits of flesh.

When the British barrage let up, German machine-guns dominated the battlefield, slowly, methodically sweeping the waves of slowly walking men. The Prussian machine-gunners were astonished

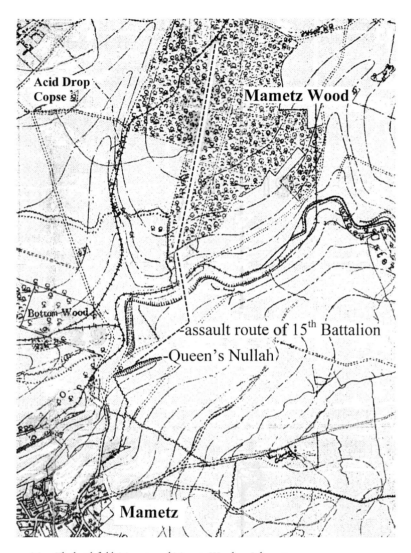

41. Map: *The battlefield, Mametz and Mametz Wood, 10 July 1916*

to see them walking slowly and thought them mad but were grateful for such easy targets and the time to aim carefully at the nearer ones. Especially ravaged were the Welsh to the right. Jones's battalion was somewhat sheltered from the full effect of machine-guns by a fortunate alignment of ground. Nevertheless, owing to artillery and machine-gun fire, a third of them fell (*IP* 163).[18]

Reaching the southern edge of the wood, Jones and the other survivors rushed the first German trench. Reaching it, he tripped and fell but did not, as he expected, receive a bayonet in the back, since the trench was occupied largely by corpses.* He and the other survivors regrouped in the trench and advanced. The dense and broken wood was nearly impenetrable with its tangle of shell-torn tree-tops and branches.[19]

Machine-guns rattled, shells burst, tree-branches crashed to the ground. In the midst of the confusion, quite close by, an unknown corporal with a very English face – 'slim, pale-complexioned, blue-grey eyes, a slight moustache, fair hair, in a state of great excitement' – shouted in a suburban, public-school voice, 'REMEMBER YOUR NATIONALITY!' and a large South Welshman also close by remarked, '*What* nationality?' Fifty-five years later, Jones vividly remembered this Welshman's 'deep-set very dark eyes' and 'tight lips . . . indicative of irony or amusement' and the slow 'solemn or mock-solemn' speech with which he added that when working a coal-face and hearing the rumble of a cave-in which might block their route to the pit-shaft, 'a lot of bloody use it would be for anyone to say "Remember your nationality"', and he concluded, 'who did that "Kiss me Hardy" little chap reckon he was?'[20]

Fighting forward until 9 in the morning, Jones and the others pushed their way 600 yards to the southern ride. From north-west of the wood, however, enfilading machine-gun fire pinned them down. In *In Parenthesis*, he would write:

---

* For certain personal details, such as this, I rely on *In Parenthesis* (p.167). Whenever I asked Jones whether an experience of the poem's John Ball happened to him, he said that it had.

they could quite easily train dark muzzles
to fiery circuit
and run with flame stabs to and fro among
stammer a level traversing
and get a woeful cross-section on
stamen-twined and bruised pistilline
steel-shorn of style and ovary
leaf and blossoming
with flora-spangled khaki pelvises
and where rustling, where limbs thrust—
        from nurturing sun hidden,
late-flowering dog-rose spray let fly like bowyer's ash,
disturbed for the movement
for the pressing forward, bodies in the bower
where adolescence walks the shrieking wood   [170–1]

Word was passed along, 'he's got a machinegun somewhere on the left'. They laid low for the rest of the morning, suffering casualties from British heavy artillery falling short.[21]

By 1 p.m., flanking enemy machine-gunners had been eliminated, and Jones and those with him began again fighting forward towards the northern ride. He saw a German accidentally drop a grenade and subsequently throw another over the bush in which Jones was hiding. In response, he threw one of his own, wounding or killing the man. He then examined the German's 'dropt stick-bomb', admiring 'the coloured label on the handle' – even battle could not suppress the aesthete in him. He considered taking the grenade as a souvenir but decided against it (IP 169).

Lack of water was becoming a serious problem. 'Terrible thirst' afflicted him and his companions. He was approached by at least one man begging for water. When water bottles were gathered to be taken back for refilling, he felt 'a good bit of reluctance' to hand his over because he expected that many of them, slung together, would be punctured by bullets on the way to the British line and back again.[22]

In the midst of the fighting, he overheard one impeccably dressed, remarkably unperturbed brigade staff-officer say with the incongruous nonchalance of social privilege to another impeccably dressed, unperturbed staff-officer, 'I say, Calthrop, have a bite, this dark French chocolate is really quite edible.'[23]

After much confused fighting, in which the struggle moved forward and back, reinforcements from the 115th Brigade arrived, and, with them, they pushed past the second, northern forest ride. As they crossed it, Jones saw haggard enemy prisoners resembling sleep-walkers – the battalion would capture over 80 that day, among them officers, whose long-skirted field-grey great-coats – 'with bits of red-piping of exactly the right hue & proportion' – he could not help admiring.[24]

He and his companions continued pushing forward. By 6 in the evening, they were within 40 yards of the northern edge of the wood, where they came under heavy rifle- and machine-gun fire from the German second line. A captain brought orders to fall back 250 yards. Retreating, Jones passed the corpses of men he had known, some mutilated beyond recognition but wearing on their sleeves the yellow badge of his battalion.

In the dark, disoriented, he was terrified by strange noises. He began stalking what he assumed was a German and recognised just in time that he was Major Jack Edwards, recently promoted to second-in-command of the battalion. Jones and those with him then began shooting separately and blindly into the vegetation until an inexperienced corporal from headquarters ordered them into line behind a thick tangle of trees from which they fired together from the prone position. Here they attempted to dig in. As they laboured, a companion was shot, and Jones tried to stop the bleeding. He later wrote in the manuscript of *In Parenthesis* that 'he'

does what he can with his First Field Dressing only he does not [know] a bloody thing about bandaging & its all abung & the blood jets impossibly fast . . . & him screaming when you go near – let alone try to cut away the saturated khaki and Mr Trever telling you to leave him to the S.B. [stretcher bearer] & get back to your digging but he dies in your arms.*

With the help of captured German picks, they managed to dig a shallow trench (which remains visible in the wood today). Here, in the continuing roar of barrage and counter-barrage, they prepared to hold for the night. Regimental Engineers arrived to string barbed wire under cover provided by a single machinegunner. The water-party arrived, with a disappointing number of bottles punctured, and thirst continued to torment them.[25]

It was probably after midnight when he was sent in a north-westerly direction to help clear a portion of the wood.‡ While advancing in pitch darkness, he was suddenly slammed hard in the left leg and went down. He thought a large shrapnel-severed branch had smashed his calf but found that he could pull himself upright and then, feeling the warm flow of blood and realizing that the bludgeoning violence had been a mere bullet, fell again.[26]

Unable to stand to walk, discarding his pack but keeping his gas-mask and rifle, he began crawling – and found he could only barely crawl – back toward the British trenches. His rifle swung off his back, hung round his neck, and, lengthened by its bayonet, impeded his progress through the bush, and then its strap got tangled in his helmet. He discarded his rifle, the intricate tool he had cleaned and oiled daily for seven months and knew from others by its bias and the flaw in the grain above the lower sling-swivel. Leaving it, he felt 'a sense of shame and . . . real affection', which he would later compare to 'the feeling of leaving a mate . . . or as when a child has to leave a toy it has had affection for'.[27]

Before long he met a Welsh corporal from his battalion, who

---

* Handwriting and omissions suggest that he wrote this passage quickly, in a sort of frenzy, reliving what he remembered. In another version, the wounded man was shot in the genitals, castration being the maiming that most soldiers especially dread. Cf. IP 174.

‡ His later estimates of the time varied from 11 p.m. to 'sometime round about 2 a.m.'

hoisted him onto his back and carried him. Major Edwards came upon them and told the corporal, 'Drop the bugger here' for stretcher-bearers to find. If every wounded man were to be carried back, their fire-power would be cut in half. 'Don't you know there's a sod of a war on?' The question amused Jones even as he was being lowered to the ground. He resumed crawling, in the dark passing and sometimes touching bodies and body parts, until he was found by stretcher-bearers, who carried him back through the open, dangerous valley of approach, which was still being heavily shelled by enemy artillery.[28]

They took him to a forward dressing-station north-east of the village where his wound was cleaned and bandaged. He had been shot in the calf muscle half-an-inch behind the bone. The medical orderly exclaimed, 'What a beautiful blighty!' (In 1937, the children of friends would call to him: 'Dai, Dai, show us your bullet wound', and he would stoop and roll up his right trouser-leg. 'What did it feel like to be shot?' they would ask, and he would say, 'It was like being hit with an iron bar', and then add, 'I was so glad I'd got a blighty one.') Though it was a flesh wound, the bullet had been fired at close range, striking at near muzzle velocity – his leg was one livid bruise from hip to toes. The bullet had not exited the leg. After its extraction, the orderly gave it to him, S.A.A., from a rifle or machine-gun, which he kept to give to his father.[29]

As the sky was growing lighter, he was loaded into 'a very hot' motor ambulance, from the window of which he saw once more the rubble of Mametz village with its large incongruous roller. He was delivered to a casualty clearing station ten miles behind the lines and placed on a trestle bed under a large marquee where, after nearly 20 hours of combat at the end of a nearly sleepless week and although the heat was extreme, he slept. He was startled awake by a cultivated, upper-class nurse asking how he felt. Her voice seemed to him 'the nicest thing in the world' – the first female English voice he had heard in seven months. It 'brought back a '"civilised" world' he had 'almost forgotten existed'. In later years he remembered that voice as having left 'an indelible mark' on him, and speculated about it possibly having made him sensitive 'to a rather exaggerated extent' to the power of 'a certain sort of voice as if it were a *physical touch* – a healing thing it is almost'.[30]

Every July for the rest of his life, he would relive in memory his experience at the Somme, saying in 1971, 'my mind can't be rid of it'.[31]

Later, in hospital, he would receive a letter from Poulter describing the relief of the battalion in Mametz Wood at 10 a.m. on the 11th and relating how Colonel Bell 'looked wonderful' in his battle-torn tunic, with unshaved face and long stick 'like a shepherd's crook', walking at the head of the column. The battalion had lost over a third of its men: 28 killed, 144 wounded, 8 missing, most if not all of the latter blown to bits. On the afternoon of the 11th, Poulter later told him, the battalion moved south to Hebuterne to spend a week burying the dead of the Irish regiments that had suffered terrible losses there.[32]

NOTES TO CHAPTER 4

1   To Tom Burns, 2 July 1971; *IP* MS; Bailley, 'The Front Line'.

2   To Harman Grisewood, 18 February 1960; to René Hague, 27 September 1974; to Harman Grisewood, 12 December 1966; to Tom Burns, 2 July 1971.

3   DJ in conversation with author, 24 August 1972.

4   The places en route listed here, which differ from that given by Colin Hughes (p. 171), are those given in the battalion diary.

5   To René Hague, 2 July 1935.

6   DJ in conversation with author, 9 September 1972.

7   Hughes, p. 172.

8   *DGC* 29; *IP* 141–3 – Jones told me that the conversation between these friends is presented in the poem as he remembered it; *IP* MS; to René Hague, 27–30 September 1974. The photos reproduced in figs. 38 and 40 came into Jones's possession after the war.

9   Hughes, p. 174.

10   To David Blamires, 6 November 1966.

11   Peter Chasseaud, *Topography of Armageddon, a British Trench Map Atlas of the Western Front 1914–1918* (Lewes: Mapbooks, 1991), p. 180.

12   Hughes, p. 175.

13   Hughes, p. 174.

14   DJ's annotations to Munby, p. 16; Munby and DJ's annotation, p. 18.

15   To Miss [Jane] Carver, 29–30 June 1972; to Nancy Sandars, 11 July 1972.

16   To René Hague, 27 September 1974; DJ interviewed by Jon Silkin, 1971. Cf. *IP* 160.

17   DJ in conversation with author, 31 August 1972.

18   To René Hague, 27 September 1974.

19   Hartrick, *A Painter's Pilgrimage*, p. 7.

20   To Tom Burns, 2 July 1971.

21   *IP* 168; Griffith, 220; to René Hague, 14 June 1970.

22   To René Hague, 4 March 1974; *DGC* 231; to Colin Hughes, draft 25 November 1969.

23   DJ to Blissett, p. 64; *IP* 173. When telling the story, DJ could not remember the name of the man addressed or precisely what kind of food he had offered.

24   *IP* 170; to Harman Grisewood, 31 December 1971.

25   Hughes, p. 21; DJ marginal note in Hartrick, *A Painter's Pilgrimage*, p. 7 (Hartrick mistakenly identifies Edwards as DJ's colonel); *IP* 172; to Tom Burns, 2 July 1971; *IP* 175.

26   René Hague, *David Jones* (Cardiff: University of Wales Press, 1975), p. 50; to René Hague, 10 July 1935; 27 September 1974.

27   DJ marginal note in Hartrick, *A Painter's Pilgrimage*, p. 7; *IP* 184; *DGC* 259.

28   To René Hague, 27 September 1974; Griffith, p. 210; to René Hague, 10 July 1935.

29   DJ's annotations to Munby, p. 19; to Harman Grisewood, 14 February 1938; DJ to Blissett, p. 139; Michael Hague, interviewed 10 September 1989; *Manchester Guardian*, 11 February 1972; Philip Hagreen to author, 9 October 1985; Tony Hyne, interviewed June 1985.

30   To Saunders Lewis, 14 July 1970; to Colin Hughes, 5 December 1970; to Alan Lascelles, 27 June 1964; *DGC* 175. Three months later, also having been wounded in Mametz Wood, Lance-Corporal Adolf Hitler would have a similar experience, waking to hear a nurse speaking his native language.

31   To Tom Burns, 2 July 1971.

32   To René Hague, 4 March 1974; DJ's annotations to Munby, p. 19; to René Hague, 27 September 1974.

CHAPTER 5

RECUPERATION

On 15 July while he was waiting to be taken to England, a 'jolly nice fair-haired' Canadian nurse kissed him said, 'You ought to be in kindergarten.' When she asked how he managed to get attested, he told her he was 20, and she said, 'You can't kid me.' That night, in the hospital ship *St David*, he crossed the Channel to England and in the morning was moved to hospital in Birmingham. There he donned the blue flannel uniform and red necktie of a military patient. On 20 July, he was sent to the idyllic Warwickshire village of Shipston-on-Stour to convalesce in Park House Hospital at 40 Church Street (fig. 42). It was one of several Georgian houses with Victorian façades on the north edge of the village. Behind it was a long garden extending

42. *Park House Hospital, Shipston-on-Stour, 1916*

to the tiny River Stour and, beyond that, rolling farmland. Encouraged to get air, he and other convalescents strolled and were served tea on the large back lawn – an experience reflected in his war epic where men recovering from wounds are imagined walking 'beside comfortable waters' (*IP* 186). And they visited the Red Lion pub down the street. Shipston-on-Stour was, as he would remember, 'an almost archetypal English village', 'a heavenly place'.[1]

It was especially heavenly for him because the hospital was staffed by unregistered Voluntary Aid Detachment nurses, one of them named Elsie Hancock (fig. 43), with whom he fell in love. Slightly older than he, she was tall, shapely, and natural. Although, as she told him, she was already engaged to an officer who had earlier recovered from a leg-wound, she felt considerable affection for him and, during his time at the hospital, gave him three photographs of herself. They spoke together frequently. In late July, he beckoned her to his side to show her a discovery: in the 22 July issue of the *Illustrated London News* was a large photograph of the ruins of Mametz showing the incongruous metal roller he had noticed several times while passing through the village (ch. 4, fig. 39). She was, he later said, 'the object of my adoration', 'heavenly', 'a wonderful girl', but 'it wasn't a real love affair' – there was no opportunity for embracing.[2]

His family visited, and he learned that the husband of his newly married cousin Gladys had been killed at the Somme. His mother visited, bringing a young neighbour from Brockley named Elsie Levitt, in whom he had shown romantic interest before enlisting. He was polite,

43. *Elsie Hancock, 1916*

they chatted, but he was annoyed, and, taking his mother aside, said, 'Why on earth did you bring her?' Another Elsie had replaced Levitt in his affections, and having the two Elsies together in the same place was disconcerting.[3]

Patients were forbidden to visit the homes of nurses, but, one afternoon in September, he and Elsie Hancock went for tea to her house, which was next door at number 36. They sat with her mother in lawn chairs under the shade of a large tree – he insisted on not sitting in the sun. Mrs Hancock offered them strawberries and cream, which he could not refuse in these circumstances but loathed to the point of nausea. Elsie was on duty that evening, so the party ended early, and, after saying goodbye to one another in the hall of the house, he and Elsie returned separately to the hospital.

The next morning Dr McTaggart, a Scots Presbyterian who ran the hospital, astonished him by delivering what he later described as the most awful, arrogant, moralistic, generalising speech he ever heard. Beginning with the Ten Commandments, McTaggart progressed to 'the inflexible laws governing the universe', Jones wondering all the while 'what he was bloody well talking about'. McTaggart concluded: 'The world is subject to certain principles ordained to be obeyed, the hospital was also subject to certain regulations, and you have broken one of them by visiting the home of Nurse Hancock.' McTaggart had hoped to keep him longer, he said, and, although he would not release him until professionally satisfied that he was fit, he now felt compelled to discharge him back to his unit soon.* Asked to comment, Jones said that he had thought the rule unimportant and asked how the doctor had received this information. McTaggart refused to disclose his source.

Before leaving the hospital four or five days later, Jones had a chance to speak with Elsie, who told him that the doctor's daughter, the hospital matron, had seen them in the garden from a top-floor window. She was jealous of popular, pretty Elsie but since Elsie was a good nurse and indispensable, he alone would suffer for their trans-

---

* About the doctor's belief in 'the inflexible laws governing the universe', Jones later commented, 'Probably isn't true, anyway.'

44. *David Jones*, Lancelot and Guinever, 1916

gression. He was bitterly angry at the informer. Fifty years later he would say with considerable passion, 'Christ forgive me, I could wring her bloody neck.'[4]

During his convalescence or subsequent sick-leave, he made a brightly-coloured pastel drawing of a knight in body-armour bearing a damsel on his charger (fig. 44), subsequently known in Jones's family as *Lancelot and Guinever*. With prominent chin, the knight clearly resembles the artist. His mother would say, 'That's David and Elsie', meaning Elsie Levitt, but Levitt's hair was black, and the damsel's hair resembles the reddish chestnut hair of Elsie Hancock, whom the damsel facially resembles (though Elsie was buxom as this damsel seems not to be).[5] The picture commemorates his love for her. The following year, he gave it to his sister as a wedding present.

Throughout the rest of the war, he and Elsie Hancock wrote to each other, and she sent him seven photographs of herself. Apart from these, all that survives of their correspondence is a picture postcard of Church Street and the hospital, with Elsie's house beyond it (fig. 42). On the reverse she writes,

> 9.8.17 Very many thanks for your letter, glad to hear you were still awfully fit. Am off to B[anbury] on Tuesday. I will drop you a line from there. The P.C. you will doubtless recognise, quite good don't you think so? am awfully busy at the Hospital, fifty up. I am in the kitchen with Miss Pratt.
> All good luck
> Yrs. E G H

Although this hardly seems fuel for erotic fantasy, he doubtless daydreamed about her – as his fictional infantrymen would daydream about their sweethearts (IP 69). He may have envied her fiancé, as does

45. 'On leave from France, autumn 1916'

one of his fictional privates, fantasising about his girl attending a fire-works exhibit with a rival, 'their closer bodies / cloaked in advantageous dark between the festive flaring' (*IP* MS), although Elsie's fiancé, too, was at the front. Thoughts of Elsie would console him for the rest of the war.

Upon expulsion from the paradise of Shipston-on-Stour, he received two weeks' post-convalescent leave. It was now autumn. Passing through London on his way to his parents' home and still wearing hospital blue, he visited A. S. Hartrick, who was now teaching at Southampton Row. Jones recounted to him the assault on Mametz Wood as a sort of comedy.[6] Hartrick suggested that he draw a picture of it for *The Graphic*. Jones went on to his parents' home. Since his father and sister worked during the week, his leave was largely a reunion with his mother. She asked him, they all asked him, about the war. He probably made light of circumstances at the front, as he had with Hartrick, but it was plain that he had suffered a great deal. She took him to have his picture taken, a photograph showing eyes

46. David Jones,
Close Quarters,
'The Assault on
Mametz Wood',
The Graphic, *9*
September 1916

that had seen too much. They are sunken, and, to the left of his left eye, wrinkles are visible that had not been there before (fig. 45).

While at home, he made and delivered the drawing Hartrick had asked for, which was published while he was still on leave, on 9 September, under the caption 'Close Quarters: a Feature of Old-Time Warfare that Survives' (fig. 46). Beneath the caption are words that probably reflect his conversation with his former teacher:

> It may be said that the nearer the belligerents the more closely do they approach the conditions of Napoleon's day, until, in hand-to-hand conflict, the difference ceases to exist. This sketch, showing the entrance of Mametz Wood by the Welsh Division – helmeted like their ancestors at Agincourt – is by a private in the Royal Welsh [sic] Fusiliers, who was wounded during the engagement.

The drawing is realistic in the mode of the boys-adventure style of illustration typical of *The Graphic* but sophisticated in design. Structurally it is divided in two with strong diagonal impulses and contrasting light and dark axes: dark in upper left and lower right corners, light in lower left and upper right corners. As soldiers move from left to right into the darkness of the wood, one of them crumples and falls backwards. Contrasting movements of advance and collapse are perpetually fixed in the diagonal criss-cross suggested by slanting grass, smoke, and the lines of rifles and bayonets. The only indication of the presence of the enemy is a fallen German helmet in the centre foreground. Barely visible in the lower right is the signature 'DAVID JONES'.

Also while on leave, he wrote and gave to his parents an essay entitled 'A French Vision'. It is his earliest surviving writing and the only contemporary written record of his thoughts and feelings about his early combat experience. His father had it typed and proofed it for publication in the *Christian Herald*, correcting the punctuation and many spelling errors – though it was not, in the end, published – and he proudly sent a copy, on 19 October, to Lloyd George. Here is David Jones's essay, written at the age of twenty:

A French Vision
(By a one-time Art Student, now in the R.W.F.)

IS IT WORTH IT?

How often this question comes with ever-increasing persistency to the intelligent fighting-man in France.

The Battalion is new to the line – just come from England; it is the first night of going into the trenches. At last, after months of training, face to face with the actualities of war. In single file, one finds oneself trudging along a desolate road – broken ruins stand grim and piteous against the dim light of the evening. One had seen numerous pictures – photos – ever since one was a child of the desolation caused by war – here at last was the actual thing. These grim ruins – these smashed, wrecked homesteads – were once, only a few months back, comfortable 'homes' – contented and happy peasants loving every corner of them.

IS IT WORTH IT?

At this moment the man in front – your chum with whom you have shared company since enlistment – drops without a sound. One had never seen a man die before, perhaps. There is a momentary halt, and the Sergeant mutters, 'Only a stray'. Again there comes the voice: '*Is it worth it?*'

This is a dangerous thought – it suggests 'giving up', it suggests something 'un-British'. But the trench is knee-deep in mud and slush – the wind is biting cold – overcoat, tunic, shirt, are soaked through – very little to eat. The man carrying the rum was shot in the communication trench, and that warming spirit has helped to strengthen, and perhaps in some measure to disinfect, the water of the trench drain. Hands are frozen; eyes are craving for rest, and weary with watching. There is sandbagging to be done, parapets to be built; enemy artillery is active and accurate. 'Is it worth it?'

A young lieutenant passes, new from Woolwich Royal Academy. He looks cold and 'fed up', probably thinking of that charming little enchantress safely ensconced in a warm drawing-room in the suburbs. As he passes he mutters half audibly, 'Damn this war! Why the ＿＿＿ did *I* join the Army?' *'Is it worth while?'* Then down the trench comes E＿＿＿, of L＿＿＿, of ＿＿＿ 'Varsity fame: 'Hallo, old fellow! Awful bore, this war; what! I was in the middle of a volume entitled 'War is the necessary Forerunner of Peace and Civilization in All Ages' by Professor ＿＿＿, that talked a lot of drivel about the 'Purifying Fire' of war etc. I'll know what to do with that wretched collection of piffle when I get back, providing the 'Purifying Fire' lets me!'

Evidently, one thinks, both these chaps think it is NOT worth while! It is an awful business, this wretched devastation, this wholesale butchery. If one had lived in the old days, war was so different then! And one mentally pictures a sunlit valley, massed squadrons of emblazoned chivalry with lances couched; and behind, bowmen armed 'cap-a-pie' with short sword and buckler. Suddenly the bowmen, with a fierce and mighty cry, charge madly to the valley, and the arrows fly thick and fast! The imagination carries one away, it is so fine. How grand to have lived then, to have heard the stirring fanfare of the heralds' trumpets, to have seen the pennons dancing in the sunlight!

． ． ． ． ． ． ． ． ． ．

And now the vision passes. Night falls, and another, and far different scene presents itself. The same valley lit by the pale moon; the groans of the wounded and dying break the silence.

'Was it worth while for these men',
five centuries, maybe, ago. By their fierce conflict, and their outpoured blood, they freed the land from the tyrant's yoke!

Worth while? Perchance Europe in thraldom still would be,

but for that battle on that sunlit day. And but for the holding of that trench – but for the blood spilt – the ruined homes – the stricken hearts of thousands – but that *one* stood in that muddy trench in cold and misery – but that the young lieutenant, 'so bored', had left the vision in the drawing-room to cry her eyes out, perhaps – but that the 'Varsity man had left his books – Europe to-day might lie prostrate 'neath the iron heel of the Teuton terror. Yes, it was worth while, after all. One wakes from the dream with the sudden command of a cockney Sergeant: 'Now then, you! relieve that man on sentry-go. Ye're late orlready!' And one goes to his post to watch for marauding Huns – goes with the smile of contentment. The trench is still cold and wet; eyes still ache, and hands freeze. But it's worth it!

Earnest, immature, lacking historical sophistication and political perspective, he writes as though trying to convince himself. He later confessed that in the trenches he was young for his age and, unlike Wilfred Owen, believed 'the old lie.'[7] But Private Jones is doing what soldiers have always done in time of war, anesthetising himself through euphemism, limited vocabulary, and comforting cliché. The analogy with the Battle of Agincourt was not original to him. The previous year had been the 500th anniversary of Agincourt, which the newspapers had compared to the Second Battle of Ypres, repeatedly asserting similarities between the current conflict and the French campaign of Henry V. The analogy pervaded the consciousness of men at the front and later informed their memoirs.

Despite its naïve jingoism, Jones's essay has remarkable affinities with *In Parenthesis*, which implicitly corrects it. The poem also begins with the night-time journey through a flooded communication trench to the front line. In the essay, modern and medieval warfare differ except in motive. In the poem, no mention is made of motive, but correspondence between modern and medieval warfare is pervasive. In the poem, allusion is particularly made to Agincourt through references to *Henry V* but in a way that contradicts, rather than endorses, the nationalistic warmongering of Shakespeare's play. In the essay, the valley charged by bowmen with short swords (like the short-sword bayonet) resembles the valley immediately before Mametz Wood, where (though unnamed in the poem) the assault that concludes *In Parenthesis* takes place. The essay is moralistic propaganda, certainly not poetry, but it is the seed of Jones's poem of the Great War.

In London, he was dismayed by civilian inability to comprehend life in the trenches. He later said, 'When I came home on leave I could hardly endure it at all because you couldn't make people understand anything.' And what interested civilians meant little to him. The Easter rebellion in Dublin was, for example, frequently discussed. When asked by relatives what 'the loyal Irish in France' thought of it, he replied curtly, 'Most of them I knew are dead.'[8] After the deep sharing and common understanding between men at the front, incomprehension at home was painful. It may have been partly to escape civilians asking questions that he visited the zoo; some months later, in the trenches, he would draw from memory a lynx he had seen there. Ambiguous and curiously unsettling, leave was further complicated by sadness at its drawing to an end.

Shortly before he was to return to the front, his mother asked him to visit his Great-Aunt Mockford in Rotherhithe. He tried to back out but she insisted, 'Oh, she'd *love* it', and he obediently went. Because it was a Sunday, the great-aunt was dressed grandly in black watered silks with lace frills and a bonnet. She said to him, as he later remembered,

> Well, David, I hear you've been fighting the Prussians. Big-boned men are they not? We thought they were in the right last time and the French in the wrong and badly led as well, but now they tell me the Prussians are in the wrong and that we must summon all our British courage and help the French to beat them. Your dear mother tells me in a letter that you were wounded fighting the Prussians . . . in a wood

and will soon be back again with your regiment, which is quite right for that is a soldier's duty – but I still think the Prussians were in the right in the other war, though I suppose they are in the wrong in this one.

He was amused to hear the Franco-Prussian War of 1870 referred to as 'the last war'. His great-aunt seemed to think hc had contended 'blade to blade with great blond Prussians of the Bismarck era'. She was, he thought, the 'nicest thing' about his leave, much better than 'the sort of questions you couldn't answer because of disparity of experience'. When he described this visit to Allen, Poulter and his other mates, they were much amused, and one of them said, 'Suppose the old girl reckoned you spent half your time knocking out bloody great Goliath-sized Jerrys with perfectly aimed sling-stones.'[9]

NOTES TO CHAPTER 5

1 *DGC*, 250; to Harman Grisewood, 11 July 1958; DGC 258; Anthony Hyne, 'Military Service', typescript, n.d.; to Harman Grisewood, 30 June 1972; to Helen Sutherland, 3 November 1952; DJ, interviewed by Peter Orr, summer 1972.

2 To Janet Stone, 7–8 July 1972; DJ interviewed by Peter Orr, early 1970s; *DGC* 258.

3 DJ interviewed by Peter Orr, summer 1972; Stella Wright, interviewed 21 June 1989.

4 DJ interviewed by Peter Orr, 1970s; to Harman Grisewood, 30 June 1972; DJ interviewed by Peter Orr, summer 1972; to Janet Stone, 7–8 July 1972.

5 Miles and Shiel repeat the mistake of DJ's mother in identifying the woman in the picture as Elsie Levitt (p. 215).

6 Hartrick, *A Painter's Pilgrimage*, pp. 233–4; on the back of the photograph, DJ writes, 'On leave from France 1916, Autumn'.

7 Letter from Lloyd George's secretary to James Jones, 25 October 1916; the text of DJ's essay corrected by his father was published in *London Magazine* 33 (April–May 1993), pp. 73–9. Printed here is the original typescript, subsequently located. As much as clarity allows, I restore DJ's punctuation, which consists largely of dashes and I delete the sometimes substantial insertions made by his father, who gave it the title, 'A Letter to His Parents'. DJ to Blissett, p. 122.

8 DJ interviewed by Jon Silkin, 1971; John Montague, 'From *The Great Bell*', *David Jones: Man and Poet*, ed. John Matthias (Orono, Maine: National Poetry Foundation, 1989), p. 82.

9 DJ in conversation with author, 4 June 1971; to Harman Grisewood, 9 October 1971; to René Hague, 27 September 1974. The great-aunt's remarks are given as DJ remembered them, in conversation with the author.

CHAPTER 6

YPRES SECTOR, THE SURVEY, PASSCHENDAELE

Jones returned to France in late October 1915, joining his battalion in the Boesinghe sector just north of Ypres, near Poperinghe. This was the extreme northern end of the British line and its area of most concentrated violence. On both sides, the men were continually pounded by artillery and trench mortars. The earth was pockmarked, grey, utterly barren – it was the most desolate area on the Western Front. Upon reporting to Battalion Headquarters, he was unhappy to learn that he had been transferred from B Company to D Company and so would be separated from intimate friends.[1]

Near headquarters he met Poulter (fig. 1), who had secured from the regimental sergeant-major permission for him to delay joining his new company. To celebrate Jones's approaching twenty-first birthday, he had stolen rum and bottled cherries from officers' supplies. The best thing about the party was Poulter, whose sense of humour and nonchalance always made Jones grin. Poulter also greatly amused himself. He had what the French call *fou rire* and at a certain point would convulse in uncontrollable laughter.[2]

There was more to John Gustav Leslie Poulter than hilarity and athletic ability. He was sensitive, cultivated, and widely read in English and French literatures. A gifted linguist, he read Greek and

47. Leslie Poulter, c. 1916

Latin easily, and was fluent in French and in Welsh, which he had learned since enlistment. After a childhood spent in Ealing, London, and Southsea in Hampshire, he had studied at Dover College, where he won prizes in language and literature. He then went to Switzerland to learn watch-making in a company owned by his godfather (who was probably also his father). Poulter was middle-class, but his values and manners were those of a conventional upper-class clubman, 'the kind of bloke', said Jones, 'who would have "dressed for dinner" had he been alone in some bloody jungle'.[3] Although English in manner, he was also the most broadly European person of his generation whom Jones knew.

During their celebration he told Poulter how he had disliked leave, and Poulter related his own experience of having to sleep on the floor while at home on leave because bed was too comfortable. He told Jones much of what had happened to the battalion during his absence, including a successful raid by 65 of its members (at the cost of 12 casualties) in the preceding week. Like Jones, Poulter had been urged to become a lieutenant and he too would have preferred being something grander. It may have been during this birthday celebration that he gave Jones a joke-application for promotion to colonel. Only part of the document survives, which includes attestations by fictional referees: 'He was born to lead. He has traits in his character which would be I consider indispensable for such a position. e.g. He is a strong Imperialist. Enthusiastic. Keen perception & wonderful memory, & is always alert. . . . I think there are few men of his age who have travelled as he has done. To my knowledge he has visited U.S.A., Canada, Russia, Switzerland, France, Ceylon, Australia. He is a good conversationalist, smart in repartee, no mean linguist & good at cross-examination. I often tell him he ought to be a K.C. [King's Counsel].' Not as adamant as Jones in resisting promotion and having attended something 'better' than an art school, Poulter would finish the war as a captain.[4]

Although Jones now knew who among their common acquaintances had fallen in the assault on Mametz Wood, he found it distressing to seek out other companions no longer with the battalion. The dead and wounded had been replaced by conscripts. Fully half of the current 486 officers and men of the battalion were strangers to him. Still, he enjoyed reunions, especially one with Reggie Allen, who was haunted since the Somme by an unshakeable premonition of death.[5]

On 24 October 1916, as a member of the 14th Platoon of D Company, Jones went into reserve dugouts in the Boesinghe sector, east of the village of Brielen, a mile-and-a-half north of Ypres. These dugouts were strong, with sandbagged walls backing like caves into the south-western bank of the Yser Canal so that the surface of the water in the canal was at a level with the heads of men standing. The dugouts opened onto a little stream called the Yser Lea, across which lay plank bridges with, here and there, rustic hand-rails that he thought surprisingly humane and lovely in this 'most uninviting of areas'. Beyond the stream was the Lizerne-Ypres road, its flanking trees shattered. Exposed to enemy fire, the bridges across the canal

48. *Fatigue duty, 1917*

were shielded by camouflage hung on uprights like washing on lines. Years later he would recognise this place of dugouts in Chaucer's description of the temple of Mars in 'The Knight's Tale': a grisly place of mischance set in a dead forest of sharp and hideous stubs, a place of harsh wind, cold, dim light, sharp burning, black smoke, and frightening, grating noises.[6] For much of the coming year, this would be home.

The day after their arrival, the battalion went into the front line across from Pilckem Ridge. The pungent smell of corpses here was worse even than in the Richebourg sector – there were fewer rats in these trenches owing to abundance of corpses in no man's land. During their first four days here the battalion suffered four casualties – one killed, three wounded. On the 31st they moved into support trenches where, that evening, one man was killed, one wounded. The relative quiet allowed the men to work continually at grading and draining trenches.

He had become aware that the war had changed. The absence of friends and companions and their replacement by strangers diminished domestic intimacy, and, like all men who had lost friends, he began to insulate himself emotionally against further loss. Slaughter was now more wholesale and mechanised. Motor transport now outnumbered horse-drawn wagons. There was much more artillery, 'ours & theirs'. Ammunition-dumps lined the roads and 'rose like slag heaps on every available bit of ground', perfunctorily camouflaged with bits of foliage. Along with 'guns of every imaginable calibre', heavy platform howitzers had been brought forward. For the first time, he saw big guns facing each other and firing in the open – force having replaced cunning. There was also a change in mood. The enthusiasm apparent before the Somme was gone. Life now seemed 'an endless repetition with no foreseeable end'.[7]

Another, more irksome change was an increase in hard labour. In preparation for a major offensive planned for the following August, the General Staff had given orders to achieve a depth of defence comparable to that of the enemy. The division would spend the next ten months consolidating and improving the trench system

49. 'Lt. Williams'

and, especially, digging and building new communication trenches. Jones assumed that his division was staying so long in this sector because of its large number of mining companies – their members, mainly from the southeast mining valleys, being invaluable in the massive trench-construction.[8]

The battalion intelligence officer, Lieutenant Williams (fig. 49), learned that Jones had been an art student and, at the beginning of November, had him transferred to Battalion Headquarters, which was a dugout in the Canal Bank. Jones now slept in a little dugout of his own in the support line. During daylight hours he worked at headquarters making maps. On nights when not on patrol, he was available for fatigue duty and participated in the continuous labour of constructing, repairing and extending trenches. Most nights, however, he accompanied Williams on patrol to see if the enemy had dug any new trenches or put out new barbed wire, Jones making sketch-maps. They never encountered parties of the enemy but often saw sentries silhouetted above enemy parapets.[9] Shortly after his arrival, on 2 November, when he was at headquarters, standing sentry, or on fatigue duty or patrol, five rounds of artillery destroyed his private dugout.

Before being assigned to Battalion Headquarters, he and his companions were, as he put it, 'one whole of bedraggled ochre'. Having been a bit of a dandy, he had experienced 'brief visual pleasure' in the elegant cut of the service tunic of the lieutenant commanding his platoon and, on rare occasions when an officer from brigade or Divisional Headquarters visited, admired the whipcord riding-breeches, the laundered shirt, the superbly tailored coat with scarlet gorget patches on immaculate khaki lapels. (Always, however, his admiration had been mixed with trepidation over the reason for the visit.) Now, a private at headquarters, surrounded by sartorial elegance, he felt strongly the degradation of his own shapeless military issue. He also resented watching batmen bring officers alcoholic drinks unavailable to him as a private (see *IP* 127). He had never been so uncomfortably aware of class distinctions. Yet, shortly afterwards, when officers in the front line began dressing like privates to avoid the distinctive silhouettes that identified them as officers to the enemy, he and his fellow privates disliked the change, which made taking orders feel like being bossed by an equal.[10]

At this time, Field Survey units issued a call for men with surveying or drawing experience, and he was sent to the 2nd Field Survey Company based at Second Army Headquarters at Cassel.[11] There he

50. 'February 1917 Scherpenberg'

was tested for the mathematically accurate draughtsmanship required to make large-scale trench maps. Like most artists, he failed at this and was relegated instead to being an observer. He was sent to Observation Group B of the 2nd Field Survey Company, Royal Engineers. This group was assigned to locate enemy batteries by cross-observation, or flash-spotting, in an area seven-and-a-half miles south of Ypres. He underwent three weeks' training in survey principles, map-reading, and the operation of a Flash-Spotting Theodolite, an enlarged, elaborate version of the surveyor's scope (fig. 52). This training and his association with 'the Survey' would surface in references in his poetry to the technology of maps and surveying (e.g. *IP* 76, 172, 177; *A* 87, 115). The move to the Observation Group was fortunate for him, since it meant that he was continually in reserve areas for the harshest months of the coldest winter in twenty years.

His unit observed from three posts in the area, one a hill overlooking Ploegsteert Wood, which spread out to the south and east towards the front line a mile away. The sight stirred his romantic imagination – he would later write, 'Ploegsteert is Broceliande', the name of the enchanted forest in Britanny where Merlin was imprisoned by enchantment (*RQ* 193). From this hill, he had a nearly topographical view of a labyrinth of British trenches. The place was 'amazing', he writes, 'with a complex meander of entrenchments', more like a German trench-system than the usual British line. Hours he spent gazing down on British trenches here increased his fascination with labyrinths and would later strengthen the affinity of his visual and literary art with mazes – though he was supposed to be looking beyond to the Messines-Wytschaete Ridge and east to Warneton behind enemy lines. (He may have been reprimanded for misdirected gazing. Half a century later he would write a poem in which sentries are chastised for looking in a direction other than the one assigned [*SL* 28, 30].)[12]

He may have gone to the observation station on Mont Kemmel (Kemmelberg), 150 metres above the Flanders plain with a good view of the maze of German lines on Messines Ridge to the east. On top of

51. [on reverse] 'The mill at Neuve Eglise which we used as an OP for spotting gun flashes etc. – the building in the foreground is the estaminet'

Kemmel was a Celtic hill-fort, a circular ridge within which were the ruins of a Roman temple. This would be a place to provoke imagining of a sort later reflected in his poetry and pictures. Two miles north was the village of La Clytte, where he may have been billeted with some of the 2nd FSC. In his poetry he would commemorate the prostitute of this suggestively named village (SL 102–3). From here, in February, he drew in his sketchbook the landscape south and west towards Scherpenberg (a half-mile away beyond some woods), a village with a mill on top of a hill (fig. 51).

He spent a lot of time at the observation post in Neuve Eglise, a hilltop village two-and-a-half miles from the front line two miles west of the western point of Ploegsteert Wood. The observation post was a rickety post-mill, whose workings fascinated him. He sketched the bottom and the central post on which it was turned to face the wind. The mill was a three-minute walk from an estaminet, where they spent off-duty hours.

52. *Theodolite*

Here he made a very quick sketch of an infantryman looking through the transit of a theodolite and a finished drawing of the instrument, shiny in its metallic perfection and symmetrical gadgetry (fig. 52). Clearly he appreciated its machine-beauty but may have had it in mind decades later when writing about the absence of significance in utilitarian devices, 'I have looked for a long while / at the textures and contours. / I have run a hand over the trivial intersections' (*SL* 9).

His job here was to help plot coordinates to pinpoint German batteries along the Messines-Wytschaete Ridge so that British artillery could destroy them prior to an attack on the ridge planned for 7 June. At night, high in the mill, when he noticed a gun-flash, he took a fix on it through the transit and read, by the light of a tiny torch, the number of degrees on the dial. He then reported by field-telephone the figures together with his estimate of the size of the gun, for which he used a code employing the names of dogs – 'Foxhound baying at twenty degrees north; Great Dane barking at five degrees south.' In his war epic, he would commemorate this method of identification in a reference to 'Berthe Krupp's terrier bitch' (182). He would also project his experience as a flash-spotter into the last words of a fictional forward-observation officer saying, 'he's bumping the Quadrangle . . . X 29 b 2 5 . . . 10.5 cm. gun . . . 35 degrees left . . . (177).

Attached to the Observer Group, with more leisure than he had at any other time during the war, he wrote a letter to his vicar, Revd Edwin Davies, at St James's, Hatcham, who gave his letter to Jones's father, who, after copy-editing and typing, passed it on to the editor of *The Christian Herald*, who published a shortened version on 17 May, 1917 under the title, 'A Soldier's Letter Home'. Here is the typed original in its entirety, entitled by his father '*Somewhere on the Western Front*':

This Christmas 1916 completed my first year of 'life in Flanders'. A year ago I was just beginning to enter into the full realization of what war means to the 'foot-slogger' – the common-place private of the infantry of the Line. The beginning of 1916 was, I think, a time of hope and looking forward to all of us, military and civil – both in Flanders and Britain. We all talked with great confidence and enthusiasm of the 'Great Push'. We thought, at least most of us, that most likely 1916 would see the triumph of the Entente over the war lords of Odin. I remember quite well sitting in a very wet and particularly bad trench in the noted Richebourg sector with a chum. We were both very cold and very wet; our rations, such as they were, had unfortunately been dropped into the mud in the communication trench, so that, on the whole, the situation was far from what the official report would call 'satisfactory'. After reviewing the situation with as much philosophy and as little pessimism as was possible, we both decided that the war *could* not possibly last another winter – no one would 'stick it', we argued. We really believed that, simply because we were both so utterly 'fed up' that to *think* of many more months under similar conditions was out of the question. Yet we both have experienced, since that time, many a worse situation, and still the business continues month in and month out! Nearly a year has rolled by since the time of the latter incident – I almost said we are still in the same position, but obviously that is untrue – we are at least one year nearer peace, and certainly during the past year, although the Bosch [sic] is very far from being completely smashed, we have shown him in every way that he is, as a Tommy would say, 'up against it'.

I am fortunate enough to have recently been transferred from my battalion to a detachment doing work in connection with observation – which, of course, means that I do no duty in the Front Line and have considerably more chance of seeing things a few miles behind. I think everybody is really very interested to know whether the press accounts of Hun barbarities in Belgium and France during the 1914 advance are exaggerated or otherwise. Of course, one hears a mixture of tales and opinions concerning the matter. A few days ago I was speaking to a fairly well educated French woman, who had been in a certain town – a fairly well known place – during a terrible ten days of German rule. She told me the story of bare-faced cruelty and unheard-of arrogance in a delightfully charming broken English accent, and in such a simple fashion, that no one could have suspected exaggeration. The Crown Prince [Wilhelm] was present during part of [the] occupation, and according ot this lady's evidence, behaved in the manner attributed to him. I will not go into any details of her pathetic story, but it will be sufficient to say that in general it was identical with that the press reported. I could not help noticing the intensely French patriotic spirit with which she referred to the Bosch. Among other remarks, this one was with an abundant amount of feeling, 'We, in France, remember 1870, you English do not. Perhaps you will remember 1914–17'.

From all appearance, the better classes out here are considerably more determined concerning the war and are obviously more patriotic than the lower orders – I don't say that this *is* so, but that it appears so, in most cases. A French town just within easy walking distance of the lines is really full of interest of a very mixed nature. The curious and striking 'ancient and modern' aspect is remarkable. For instance, one sees a Market Square with a Gothic Church – its ancient embattled tower against the sky, a British plane circling above, British Staff Officers, resplendent in much brass, red tabs etc., easy-going French soldiers on leave, perhaps mud-covered Tommies straight from the trenches but usually pretty cheery, peasants with baskets of foodstuffs, Roman priests with parchment-like skin and shabby black cassocks, giving a friendly nod to passers-by – these latter seem very reminiscent of the France of long ago. It would no doubt be some surprise to the person who is perhaps familiar with pre-war France with its difficulty of language, to see to-day, on almost every other shop and house, such notices as 'Tea Room' – 'Open to English troops', 'Dinner provided here', 'Grocery and Fruit' etc. – and certainly almost every inhabitant speaking some sort of English! It is sometimes rather hard to imagine that perhaps the very house one is seated in has been the billet of German troops sometime during the last two years. Certainly other inhabitants of northern France deserve every ounce of our sympathy, indeed I always feel that even the British soldier actually out here altogether fails to duly appreciate the sacrifice of France. I fear he rather judges the French nation hardly, because some money-making inn-keeper overcharges him occasionally!

Sometimes, by way of additional interest, a batch of Bosch prisoners, seeming fairly contented with life, pass by to work. One wonders if perhaps any one of them ever saw the place of their captivity in the days when the cup of success was running over, and when, with vandal joy, they gloated over a prostrate and stricken Belgium. Naturally enough the good-humoured and humorous Tommy cannot withhold some taunting jest at the expense of the captive Hun – who usually passes on with sullen indifference! During the two years or more that have expired since the British first set foot on French soil, the English influence has gradually spread, until to-day the country seems, in some respects, like an English Colony. Naturally enough many destitute refugees from the territory now occupied by the Hun have become quite the reverse from destitute, by means of setting up small shanties behind our lines and selling coffee and all sorts of odds and ends to the British troops. Well of course one could go on writing for ever about life out here, but I think I must really finish here for the present. Give my kindest regards to everybody whom I know. Like yourselves at home, we have to live in hope that 1917 may see the end of the struggle – but of course to discuss the 'duration of the war' is worse than futile. So au revoir.

Yours very sincerely,
David Jones

During this time of greater leisure, he made about twenty drawings in his sketch book and two finished drawings for reproduction. The first of the finished drawings was printed by his father as the cover of a New Year's card (fig. 53). It displays a distressed damsel and tonsured

53. Is there Peace?, *New Year 1917*

144

monk (wearing the habit Jones had worn to be photographed at Camberwell, ch. 1, fig. 3), awaiting the outcome of a fight between two knights. Inside, Jones writes in Welsh, *A oes heddwch?* ('Is there Peace?') – the question asked three times in bardic ceremonies by the archdruid with a naked sword. When the congregation has answered *Heddwch* ('Peace') three times, he sheaths the sword. The damsel is a version of Elsie Hancock, whose photographs Jones carried with him.

The second finished drawing, made soon afterwards, reflected recent political events. In November 1916, Germany began publicly calling for an end to the war and offered to help the United States establish a League of Nations to ensure world peace. On 12 December the German chancellor sent written peace proposals. News of this gave Jones and his companions hope that their ordeal would soon be

54. 'Germany and Peace', The Graphic, 20 January 1917

145

over. On 30 December Britain and France rejected the German offer as insincere. Jones regretted this, as the second of these drawings suggests. He sent it to Hartrick, who published it on 20 January 1917 in *The Graphic* over the caption 'Germany and Peace' (fig. 54). It was drawn, according to a note published with it, 'in a dug-out by the aid of a candle'. In the picture, the alluring and vulnerable angel Peace – yet another Elsie, idealised but now also eroticised with a shoulder bared – kneels amid graves with Gothic architecture in the background. She watches with apprehension as a German knight, sporting a modern Prussian moustache, approaches with outstretched hand and lowered, loosely-held sword – a weapon visually corresponding, as well as causally related, to the graveyard crosses. On his shield is a heraldic eagle that has oppositional affinity with doves of peace flying to (and one perched on) the angel's arm. Germany's intentions seem chivalrous. As a Gothic knight, he corresponds to the symbolically positive Gothic ruins rising in the background into a light sky. The angel is anxious, however, and her anxiety is stressed by the diagonals and slanting verticals of the sword and crosses. The meaning is uncertainty: tension between fear and hope.

As a flash-spotter Jones was unsuccessful. Sometimes flash followed flash so quickly that he had to mark the second while reporting the first and he was unable to do two things at once. The mill swayed in the wind. In the dark he sometimes had difficulty finding the speaking end of the telephone. When reaching for the phone, he sometimes jogged the theodolite, moving its dial. Having lost the bearing, he made up the figures – not, he realised, a useful thing to do. By the end of February, he was discharged from the Survey Company on the trumped-up charge of not having had his hair cut. 'My association with the Engineers', he later remembered, 'was shameful and brief.'[13]

On the morning of 1 March 1917 he trudged several miles under full pack to a railhead to catch a train back to his battalion north of Ypres. Despite his protests, a transport officer insisted on putting him on a train going south-west. That afternoon he arrived at a camp on a hill above Rouen, where he was detained for nearly a month, awaiting confirmation from his battalion. In the meantime, he was sent nearby for training to the notorious Bull Ring at Étaples, 'a paradise for Staff Instructors; detested by all front-fighters'. The place specialised in 'assault drill', which he hated.[14] When approval from his battalion finally arrived, he caught a north-bound train and, with a fresh draft of new recruits, rejoined his unit in reserve. Once again he had reunions with Poulter and Allen, and he learned that, owing to nearly continuous artillery bombardment, the battalion had suffered severe casualties during his months away.

On 29 March the battalion went by train to Ypres and marched from there to the Hill Top sector of the western Canal Bank. There he drew on canvas a salvage map based on a tracing of a regular series-map of a section of the Yser Canal (fig. 55). Resembling a section of spinal cord, in brown, green, and purple inks, the map shows eight of ten bridges across the canal intact and passable. The Yser Lea flows along the west bank

55. 'Salvage Map Showing areas worked from 2.2.17 to date'

paralleling the road. The buildings and moat to the east belong to North and South Zwaanhof Farms. In four groups to the left of the canal are the dates material was deposited at salvage dumps. He kept for himself a copy of the long, abstractly beautiful map. He also kept another map, which he labelled 'Barrage Map, Pilckem, 1917'.

Stationed again at Battalion Headquarters, he was now an office-wallah, benefiting from the practice of assigning to headquarters 'old sweats', men who had been wounded, or men who had special qualifications. He could draw maps, but he was also one of the few surviving original members of the battalion, and they wanted to keep him alive for the sake of continuity. Headquarters was a little safer than anywhere else, but, while remaining attached to HQ for much of the next year, he continued to participate in the regular tour between firing, support, and reserve trenches, and reserve billets, continuing to take his turn on sentry duty and taking part in patrols, fatigues, and raids.

About this time, moving one night in pitch darkness along a communication trench, he met a man on sanitation fatigue – a 'shit wallah' assigned to empty a latrine and carrying two full buckets. The stench was strong. Just able to make out the face of Evan Evans from a rural area of Cardiganshire who belonged to one of the Welsh battalions in the regiment, Jones said, 'Hello Evan', and, offering him a cigarette, 'You've got a dirty bloody job.'

> 'Bloody job, what do you mean?'
> 'It's not the kind of work I'm particularly keen on.'
> 'Bloody job – bloody job indeed. The army of Artaxerxes was
>   utterly destroyed for lack of sanitation.'

Evans urged him to read some history, and they went on talking, but it was the start of the conversation that Jones would remember. It amused him and exemplified the difference between ordinary Welshmen, who are often learned, and ordinary Englishmen, who are not. He thought that Evans took 'comfort from the historical parallel' – a thought possibly involving projection on Jones's part, who certainly found comfort in historic parallels, which give the new an aspect of familiarity. Evans would join Lloyd George as a prototype for Dai Greatcoat at the centre of *In Parenthesis,* the archetypal soldier familiar with the past who never dies (79–84).[15]

When not in reserve billets, the men of the battalion continually trapped rats, at a rate of about 500 a month. Rats bred far faster than they could kill them, but some attempt had to be made to control their number because rats spread an infective jaundice called Weil's Disease. Abundant in no man's land owing to frequent raids, human corpses were the favourite food of rats, who preferred the eyes and liver and literally 'dug in'. But they also frequently invaded the trenches in search of garbage, boldly swarming dugouts, and scampering over the faces of sleeping men. Jones once went to sleep using his greatcoat, with biscuits in its pockets, as a blanket. At dawn he discovered the biscuits gone and holes in the pockets – rats had crawled over his body under the coat and eaten through the pocket-lining.[16] He felt little if any revulsion for rats. While with the Observer Group, he had made several sketches of a pair of rats shot as an old dugout was pulled down. One of these drawings (fig. 56.) is among the best of his war-sketches. It exhibits the sympathy that typifies his best animal drawings and suggests why he would later be considered one of the best draftsmen of animals of the century.* He would celebrate rats in his war epic where they 'sap' their 'own amphibious paradise' and 'redeem the time of our uncharity' because they feast on 'the secret parts of us' not through malice but by a rule of their nature (IP 54). As natural as corpse-stench, they were, to him, inoffensive reminders of a saner order than the one he was professionally involved in.

56. 'Nov. 1916 rats shot during the pulling down of an old dugout in Ploegsteert Wood D.J.'

* The American fiction writer, artist and critic Guy Davenport writes that as a drawer of animals 'Jones's only rival on the continent was Dufy' (letter to author, 20 December 1995).

On 18 February, while still with the Observer Group, he had written to a friend who subsequently visited Jones's parents and showed them his letter. Jones's father copied part of it onto a small piece of paper of the sort he used for scriptural admonitions which he carried to read throughout the day. Labelled 'from David' and entitled 'Extract from letter', the copied passage reads, 'I am glad you called to see my people. I often wondered how they really took the war. I thought I knew what it was to love them before I left home – *but I know now in truth*.' On the reverse of the paper are his concluding words: 'At any rate I shall see you in what our fathers called "the green fields of Avallon"'. Nothing else survives of his letters to his family. Of those he received from family members, all that remains, because he later remembered it, is a sentence his mother wrote near the end of a letter: 'Really, David, the spelling in your last letter was a disgrace to the family – a child of four would do better.'[17]

Letters from family and friends may have saved his life. One evening as he was removing his clothes, he discovered to his surprise that a ricochet bullet had penetrated the left pocket of his tunic, passing through a packet of letters and then through his cardigan,

57. Self-portrait, 1917

waistcoat, shirt, and underwear vest, just grazing the skin of his chest. He could not remember having felt the impact.[18]

Early in 1917, his steel helmet saved his life. He was in the firing trench when a mine exploded just in front of him. In the rain of debris, a large piece of metal struck his helmet, just failing to penetrate but knocking him senseless. He came to with his helmet pressed down around his ears and eyes and a herringbone pattern imprinted across the inside of it. For the next week he had a very stiff neck. After the war, Poulter, who was 6 feet 2 inches and strong, would recount Jones being struck down and he (Poulter) picking him up, tucking him under one arm, and running with him to safety.[19] This may have been that occasion. Jones would never recall being carried, but then he had been unconscious. His first war sketch in 1917 – a self-portrait, in which he appears to have a bruised eye – may have been drawn shortly after this battering (fig. 57).

Perpetually cold, he devoted much of his free time to searching for firewood. While off duty on a rainy Sunday, and wandering alone between the support and reserve lines, he came to farm buildings shattered by shelling. The wood of those buildings was too wet to burn, he knew, but nearby was a byre that seemed to have its roof intact and might contain dry, broken cartwheels, spare lumber, or even a stack of firewood. He picked his way over the broken, muddy terrain and, reaching the byre, put his eye to a crack in the paling, expecting to see in the darkness the light of an opening in another wall where he could enter. Instead he saw two gusty candle-flames. As his vision adjusted to the dark, he made out the back of a man in an alb and short gold-coloured chasuble facing a stack of ammunition boxes covered by a white cloth. On this stood the two candles. Their flames extra-gilded the chasuble and gave a golden warmth to the cloth and to the drab, muddied khaki tunics of a half-dozen infantrymen kneeling on a straw-covered floor. (The location, in a byre, may unconsciously have evoked the Nativity.) Among them were two burly privates he recognised, a Cockney Italian and an Irishman. He was especially impressed at the sight of the Irishman, a fearsome, hard-drinking fist-fighter. The tinkling of a little bell broke the silence, followed faintly by mysterious words spoken by the man in the chasuble. Jones gazed in rapture and then quietly withdrew, realizing that this was a Catholic Mass in progress.* It had seemed to him like the Last Supper. Never had he experienced at the Anglican Office of Holy Communion the unity he sensed between that priest and those men. And he was impressed at how close to the front line it was. He may later have made a drawing reflecting what he saw (fig. 58).‡ In a panorama of desolation, 'a wasted land of ubiquitous mud and rusted iron', peeking into this Chapel Perilous, he had experienced an epiphany of beauty and transcendence, a paradigmatic vision of a peace impervious to outward physical circumstance. This sight was for him 'a great marvel', something he might have read about in an ancient Celtic tale, and it would remain one of the most numinous experiences in his life.[20] He resumed his search and eventually found some wood for a fire.

On 7 April 1917, a bright, quiet day, after a gas-alert test, the men of the battalion received news that the United States had formally declared war on Germany. That night, from their reserve positions, they watched Ypres being heavily shelled little more than a mile to the south. The shelling went on for two-and-a-half hours, involving incendiary shells which, according to the battalion diarist, 'burst to fine effect'. For Jones, it was like watching fireworks at the Crystal Palace from atop a hill near his family's house. A few days later they saw enemy artillery flatten the remnant of the famous Ypres tower. On the 9th, local shelling killed three men and wounded two. On the 10th, the battalion moved north into support trenches in the central sector of the Western Canal Bank. Heavy snow transformed

---

* He later surmised that he had witnessed the part of the Mass beginning just after the elevation of the chalice and continuing through the prayer beginning *Nobis quoqui peccatoribus*, which translates, 'To us, also, your sinful servants, who hope in the multitude of your mercies, please grant some part of fellowship with your holy apostles and martyrs . . .'

‡ This drawing may be of an Anglican communion service. The priest in the drawing (fig. 58) is depicted after the *Nobis quoqui*, facing the congregation while distributing Communion.

the 45-minute walk into a five-hour ordeal. Three days later Jones's company remained in support trenches as the rest of the battalion moved forward.

At 10 a.m. on 16 April there was a gas alarm. On went the masks, and the men waited, remembering victims of gas coughing up their lungs in clots in field hospitals. Near the end of his life, Jones would tell a friend, 'The terrible thing about gas in the war was you never knew when they were going to use it. They mixed gas shells with ordinary shells. Battalion [Headquarters] had a gong – you beat it, just like announcing dinner. The brigade took it up, and then division had a terrific siren. Everybody would rush about, saying there isn't gas, yes there is.'[21]

58. *Mass*

On the 17th, in wind and sleet, they left for divisional reserve at Roussel Farm – the cold mud so deep that it took hours to pass through 400 yards of communication trench. They arrived at 3.30 a.m. On occasions such as this, he was intrigued by the closing of headquarters at precisely the moment it was opened in the new location, so that the battalion was never without a headquarters yet never had two.[22] After five days of training, they went back into support trenches on the Canal Bank, where it was quiet until 10 a.m. on the 24th, when a heavy German bombardment fell all along their front.

Expecting an attack, they waited in dugouts. He was in the firing-trench and, not having seen his friend Harry Cook all day, was worried that he might have been hit, though, as a signaller with access to whisky, Cook might also be 'tucked away dead-drunk unaware of Jerry's mounting bombardment' (fig. 59). Noticing that his platoon was low on small-arms ammunition, Jones slipped out of the firing-trench and ran towards a recess in a communication-trench wall where boxes of S.A.A. were stashed. As he ran he saw Poulter running down a trench at an angle to his own and shouted to him as loud as he could across the earth wall and against the noise of explosions, 'HAVE YOU SEEN HARRY?' Without pausing, Poulter yelled back, 'I SAW YOUNG HARRY WITH HIS BEAVER ON' – a beaver being, Jones knew, the face-guard of a medieval helmet. At once, the present conflict imaginatively became one with earlier warfare. So Cook was alive, and Jones lifted the box of S.A.A. with a light heart, but Poulter had been quoting something. It took him a while to recall the source – *Henry IV, Part I*, a play he chiefly remembered for its Welsh character Owen Glendower, of whom he was extremely fond.[23] Later he would cite Poulter's spontaneous allusion to illustrate the penetration of the

59. 'In [Ypres] Salient. Harry Cook asleep 1917'

present by the literary-historical past in the minds of soldiers during the war, something literary critics found hard to believe as realistic.

For eight of the next eleven days, the battalion was heavily shelled. On the night of 6 May, an enemy raiding party broke into the front line, killing two men, wounding three, and taking three prisoners. Jones was among those who rushed to expel the raiders. The following days were fairly quiet   a day with only one or two short periods of heavy shelling was now considered quiet. On the 10th and 12th, artillery fire fell on them sporadically all day long. Old hands informed new recruits anxious about the increased fire that 'a German attack was about as likely as getting a spot of leave', but during day-long shelling on the 14th, 'all composure vanished' at the 'unmistakable crackle of . . . "independent fire"', which meant that enemy assault troops were attacking. To him the sound was 'exhilarating'.[24] It was another raid, which he also helped repulse, resulting in eight British dead, five wounded.

In this sector at about this time, he had a memorable encounter. He was shaving very early in the morning where a communication trench joined two trenches leading to the front line. A pleasant voice from around a revetment said, 'Good morning'. Turning his head, he was astonished to see the Prince of Wales, wearing a short 'British Warm' and light woollen scarf. 'Do you happen to know', Edward asked, 'which of these trenches leads directly to' – he named a certain post – 'in the forward trench?' Embarrassed, with lather on his face and wearing a tattered waist-coat, Jones indicated the trench and advised the Prince to be careful by a certain trench-sign 'as it's exposed, sir'. Edward said, 'Thanks, can't have a fag with you – an awful hurry', and disappeared. A few minutes later, a red-faced colonel, puffing to catch his breath, stuck

60. Edward, Prince of Wales

his head round the revetment and asked, 'Have you seen Wales?' Jones said yes and that he had directed him to the forward trench. 'Why didn't you stop him?' asked the colonel, and, as the colonel ran off, Jones said, 'How could I, sir?' (The Prince was not supposed to be alone in areas subject, as this was, to violent bursts of fire.)[25] Edward's courtesy and courage stirred in Jones the affection that most infantry-men felt for him. In some respects this was an encounter of the sort that might have occurred in one of Lewis Carroll's Alice books, of which Jones was sometimes reminded while on sentry duty, scanning the local wonderland through a periscope's looking-glass. Years later he sketched Edward as he remembered seeing him (fig. 60), and the encounter would inform part of his war epic, in which 'A young man in a British warm . . . enquired if anyone had seen the Liaison Officer from Corps, as one who asks of the Tube-lift man at Westminster the whereabouts of the Third Sea Lord' (*IP* 97).

On 6 May, in a forward-post, Reggie Allen was killed by a trench-mortar projectile. Being a soldier was a job. Death and mutilation had long since ceased to appal Jones – they had become, if not normal, usual. But when a close friend was killed, friendship, which had been his chief solace, became his sharpest grief. He mourned for Reggie Allen. In 1937 he would dedicate *In Parenthesis* 'especially' to 'PTE. R.A. LEWIS-GUNNER FROM NEWPORT MONMOUTHSHIRE' – using only his initials lest 'some relative or someone who loved him might chance to see it & be upset'.[26]

In mid-May the battalion was told that it would take part in a major offensive on the Ypres front. This would be the Third Battle of Ypres, better known as Passchendaele. The battle plan represented in the High Command a renewed faith in decisive frontal attack. It was a faith undermined by failures at Second Ypres, Loos and Gallipoli, and severely shaken at the Somme, where official victory had been calamitous. Unable to develop an alternative strategy, however, the General Staff wanted to try again.

The frightfulness of artillery fire now exceeded even that at the Somme. Dawn bombardments became routine, with other irregular shelling often after long periods of quiet. On 17 June they were shelled heavily and took enormous casualties: 30 killed, 60 wounded. Heavy shelling on the 22nd caused what the battalion diarist calls 'a great amount of damage to trenches & personnel'. Artillery was now more accurate than earlier in the war, and its main target was no longer opposing artillery, as before the Somme, but infantry in the trenches. In addition to increasing casualties, increased shelling added to heavy labour, requiring constant repairing of collapsed trenches – digging them out, filling and stacking new sandbags, assembling and installing fresh revetments. Because fatigue duties were continuous, this sector was a place of dangerous hard work. On the 23 June, huddled in a dugout with others, Jones endured seven hours and fifteen minutes of continuous shelling.

Even veterans of later wars find it hard to imagine what it was like to endure such intense artillery fire so often for so long. A barrage began with the shriek of incoming shells. Muscles tensed. Explosions convulsed the air, earth flew high, and jagged shell-casing fragments whizzed and whistled – followed by the distant banging of the guns. If accurate, the first shells caught men exposed in the trenches. Realizing that this is not isolated shelling, survivors scurried into dugouts, sheltering with others inside the shuddering earth. Despite its roof of timber, corrugated iron, sandbags and covering earth, a dugout directly hit crashed like a matchbox. Men cringed with each near burst, sharing blank anticipation. A near-miss exploding before a dugout could bury men alive. Jones would remember how the near 'burst on burst of Howitzer H.E. of heavy calibre' left them shaken and aching, and made 'the sharp, brittle detonation' of lesser artillery seem, by comparison, 'trivial' (*IP* MS).

In a light bombardment, one shell a minute might land in the immediate vicinity. In a heavy bombardment, one shell landed in a company sector every two or three seconds from one field gun for every ten yards under fire and one heavy gun for every twenty yards. The bigger shells launched geysers of mud, sandbags, rocks, sometimes with gore, hundreds of yards into the air – gigantic exclamation marks, hugely cratering the earth. More dangerous over a wider area, however, was shrapnel, which arrived with (approximately) every four heavy howitzer shells, exploding like an oversize grenade in a compact cloud of thick, slowly diffusing dark smoke.[27] Every near shell-burst hurt the mind.

Then, suddenly, quiet. You heard the moaning of men; the screaming of rats; the buzzing of flies; and if you were in the reserve line, the cries or groans of terrified or wounded horses. Five, ten, fifteen minutes, then a shrieking explosion and another and the barrage descended again. In a very bad bombardment, the interval between explosions gave way to continuous crescendo. Underground in a dugout, the roar resembled an amplified tropical thunderstorm. Outside in the trench, the raging was beyond noise, an oppressive solidity you shrank from. If down below the earth shook, up above it heaved like the surface of the sea in storm. In dugouts, men stricken with claustrophobia were restrained from rushing into the maelstrom. In Jones's experience, there were 'chaps who fear being caught underground & those who fear most the nakedness of above ground'. He was among the latter, for whom the dugout was enwombing safety, the earth a protecting mother.[28]

A prolonged artillery barrage was physical and emotional torture, reducing men to aching vulnerability while it lasted. One soldier described the experience of a prolonged barrage as like being tied to a post while someone swings a sledgehammer at your head. The hammerhead whirls forward slamming, if it misses, into the post inches from your skull, sending wood splinters flying.[29] This happens again and again. The continual experience, day after day, of even light bombardments was enervating – a numbness like shock set in. Exhaustion, too, eclipsed fear or drove it beneath consciousness, leaving a sadness that lengthened into malaise. At some level of awareness, it was difficult not to take personally such an extreme manifestation of hate.

Men assigned to sentry-duty could not, as a rule, shelter from a bombardment in dugouts but had to remain in the open trench watching through periscopes for an attack. On many occasions Jones stood sentry during a barrage. Through the looking-glass, he saw the boundary between earth and sky dissolve in sudden twilight illuminated by the leaping flames of explosions transforming the waste land into a Turner seascape. It was not unusual for men to emerge from dugouts after a bombardment to find a sentry crushed under earth or blasted open or sitting as usual, his life neatly taken by the surgical slice of a shell-casing splinter.

61. 'C.O. 15 RWF'

Rifle practice, as in the first week of June at St Omer, had now come to seem futile to Jones. With the increasing dominance of artillery, his rifle had become, he thought, a counterpart to the medieval longbow. Both had transformed warfare, both were the perfected weapons of the individual, and, as the longbow had become ineffective at the end of the Hundred Years War, the rifle was now, he thought, obsolete.[30]

On 28 June, after four days of especially heavy shelling, he and his battalion left the Canal Bank for a camp in the St Hilaire area for two weeks of assault training and drilling.

On 23 July they spent the night near Tuquela Farm within 200 yards of the German line digging narrow (two feet wide, seven feet deep) assembly trenches for the coming offensive amid exploding shrapnel and falling howitzer H.E. and gas shells. In 1970 he would recall this night as 'the worst of all' because from the start they had to wear gasmasks. Colonel C. C. Norman (fig. 61), who had replaced Bell, walked up and down in the open wearing no gas mask but 'threatening blue murder on any man taking off his mask', which they desperately wanted to do. Gasmasks were 'ghastly to wear for very long', Jones recalled, 'especially if one was exerting oneself – they became a filthy mess of condensation inside & you couldn't see out of the misted-over talc of the eye-vents'. It was typical of Colonel Norman, who had already won the D.S.O., to stroll in the open amid falling shells. Like his predecessor, he was a man of 'outward calmness & immaculate attire as though he was paying an afternoon call in Belgravia' – an attitude that was, for Jones, at once amusing, morale-boosting, and '*aesthetically* right'. Among those digging

> were new recruits who had come straight from Wales. One of them was a farmer's boy; he couldn't speak a word of English.... when he'd dug his little hole he just got into it and snuggled up. You simply couldn't budge him. The NCOs kicked his backside and so on but he just wouldn't move. And it made it jolly difficult to dig the trench. The Germans . . . must have known about the digging and got the range, but the shells were falling a few yards further on, on a hedge. But this chap was absolutely petrified. Then a nice chap, Sergeant Morgan, said 'Lift him out and I'll finish the trench and then you can put him back in.' All this was in gasmasks. We dug all night. I thought this is the end; they've got us this time. But d'you know, in the morning – it was August [sic], not a long night – we found not a single person had been hit. No casualties in the whole battalion – in the whole brigade, I think.

Before dawn, as they covered the new trench with branches cut from the hedge behind it, Jones recalled the words from *Macbeth*: 'The wood of Birnam / Let every soldier hew him down a bough' (V, iv, 6). (When asked what happened to the farmer's boy, he replied, 'God knows. Probably in a couple of weeks he was a bloody good soldier – if he survived.')[31] He would be mistaken about there being no casualties. No one was killed or wounded in the ordinary sense, but for the first time in the experience of the battalion, the gas shells mixed with ordinary artillery shells contained mustard gas, a terrible surprise for some of the men, whom it blinded.

On the morning of 25 July, D Company, with Jones helping to guard the flanks, participated in a raid on Pilckem Ridge and was forced to retreat, suffering heavy casualties and 16 men taken prisoner. Two days later the whole of A Company conducted a raid in the evening. Jones was sent forward with his platoon to guard one of the flanks. The raiders advanced to find the front line empty and advanced further to the support trenches where two German battalions waited. As the night darkened, fighting was furious, and the outnumbered raiders were annihilated. The battalion diarist writes that more than 100 men were 'for the most part . . . either killed or wounded'. Jones's platoon was also 'badly cut up'.

Lazarus Black, with whom he had shared billets in Llandudno, was in the raiding party and had survived. After returning to the firing trench, he confided to Jones that he would ask for a decoration for saving an officer's life by killing a German. Jones was astounded. The night had been pitch dark, the raid disastrous. He urged Black not to make the request since word was sure to leak out and he would be a laughing stock. The next day, Black nevertheless made his appeal to the officers immediately above him, who scoffed at him but passed on his request. News of this quickly spread, and Black was ridiculed, though not as much as Jones had feared. Later, Black confided to him that he had wanted the decoration solely to make his wife and four children happy.[32]

On the night of the 30 July 1917, the regiment moved into position to initiate the battle of Passchendaele. They arrived at three in the morning. The brigade's objective was to capture Pilckem village and Pilckem Ridge up to half-way between the village and the Steenbeek River. Jones was assigned to 'battalion nuclear reserve' – a group from which the already depleted battalion could be reconstituted if it were wiped out during the assault. Upon receiving his assignment, he asked the adjutant to be removed from the list so he could take part in the

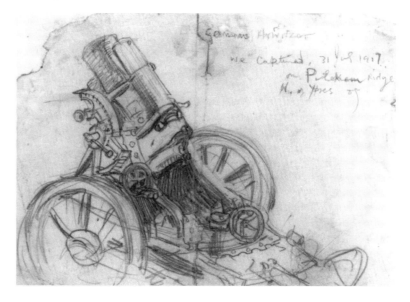

62. 'German Howitzer we captured, 31 July 1917 on Pilkem [sic] Ridge N. of Ypres. DJ'

attack.* Although he wanted merely to remain with his friends, he argued that he ought to trade places with a married man. The adjutant furiously berated him for 'pretending to wish to be a bloody hero' while knowing full well that men detailed had no choice in the matter. Simmering down, he told Jones that there would be plenty of other opportunities, that the nucleus was likely to be called upon anyway, and that he only wished he had been assigned to it. Feeling foolish, Jones tried to explain that he had not meant it that way. He was forced to endure the ignominy of relative safety. Occupying positions 'beneath the trajectory / zone' (WP 33), the 'nuclear reserve' was subject to artillery fire.[33]

Without him, his battalion moved on 31 July east to assembly trenches across the only intact canal bridge – seven bridges having been destroyed since he had drawn the salvage map five months earlier (fig. 55). They attacked at 3.50 a.m. and moved forward easily

---

* The adjutant was no longer Captain Elias, who had been killed since the Somme.

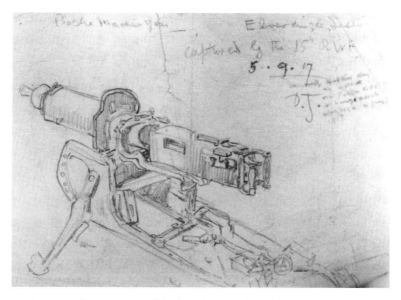

63. 'Boche Machine gun captured by the 15th RWF Elverdinghe sector 5.9.17 ... sometime during the attack on Pilekem [sic] Ridge at Langemark which began in July 1917.'

to Pilckem village, where the German Third Guards, newly arrived
and rested, met them with fierce machine-gun fire, sniper fire, and an
artillery barrage. Casualties were heavy and included most of the officers, including Colonel Norman. Keeping in formation, the remainder
struggled in deep mud past Pilckem village and concrete machine-gun
emplacements, which they outflanked, compelling their garrisons to
surrender. In reserve, listening to the gunfire, Jones worried about his
friends and bitterly regretted his separation from them.[34] Rain started
falling steadily as the battalion gained the ridge, capturing a German
howitzer and machine-gun, both of which he subsequently sketched
(figs. 62, 63). They dug defensive positions, which they held in constant
rain for a day.

Jones rejoined them by the evening of 1 August and spent the next
day helping defend their gains. At midnight on the 2nd, they withdrew
to take over the front line at Steenbeek. By the 3rd, according to the
battalion diarist, rain had turned 'the battle field into a sea of mud'

so deep they could scarcely move – this was the wettest summer in many years. On the 4th, they were relieved and returned to the Canal Bank, where they were given chocolate and cigarettes, hot food, clean clothes, and a fresh colonel, R. H. Montgomery.

Here Jones heard from the survivors of the assault, including Poulter, what they had endured and learned who among his acquaintances had fallen. Their experience scoured his imagination differently than if he had fully shared it. He would say, 'I saw enough to guess something of the assaults over a terrain of churned-up mud, water-brimming shell-craters, not a yard of "dead ground" not a fold of earth the length of your body and sighted with his usual accuracy his sweep of fire from narrow slits of concrete pill-boxes covering all approaches, & heavy mortars operating from behind each stark ridge.'[35] He may have experienced survivor's guilt, as he probably had when rejoining his battalion in March. Twenty or more years later he would write about this assault and, in the last years of his life, rework this material into publishable form as his most poignant and, paradoxically, funny mid-length poem, 'Balaam's Ass', the remarkable conclusion to his last book of poetry, *The Sleeping Lord* (pp. 97–111).

NOTES TO CHAPTER 6

1 Postcard from Elsie Hancock to DJ, 9 September 1917.
2 *DGC* 243, 230; David Poulter (Leslie's son), interviewed 11 June 1990.
3 To Harman Grisewood, 1 February 1971.
4 David Poulter, interviewed 11 June 1990, letter to author, 9 February 1990. The document quoted here was subsequently inscribed by DJ 'Leslie's poem 1916.'
5 DJ to Blissett, p. 122.
6 DJ MS frag. n.d.; to René Hague, 14 December 1973; *DGC* 251.
7 To Miss [Jane] Carver, 29–30 June 1972; DJ, *Tablet* (1 July 1966); conversation with author, 9 September 1971; to Harman Grisewood, 2 October 1964; to René Hague, 27 September 1974.
8 DJ MS frag. n.d.
9 DJ MS frag. n.d.; to Saunders Lewis, 27 April 1974.
10 To René Hague, 9–15 July 1973; MS frag. n.d.; *IP* 137; DJ in conversation with author, 24 August 1972.
11 For the operation of the FSO and information that follows about specific locations, I am indebted to Peter Chasseaud, letter to author, 8 July 1993, and his essay 'David Jones and

the Survey', *David Jones, Artist and Poet*, ed. Paul Hills (Scolar Pres: Aldershot, 1997), pp. 18–30.

12 *DGC* 243.

13 To Julian Asquith, 13 November 1939.

14 *IP* MS; *IP* 219 n12; *DGC* 242-3; 'David Jones – Maker of Signs'.

15 *IP* 207 n37; to René Hague, 11 August 1974; to Saunders Lewis, 19 November 1954; DJ interviewed by Peter Orr, 1972.

16 To Valerie Wynne Williams, 3 November 1962.

17 To Tony Hyne, 19 June 1974.

18 To René Hague, 1 January 1973.

19 David Poulter, interviewed 11 June 1990; to René Hague, 1 January 1973.

20 DJ quoted by Hague, *David Jones*, p. 58; *DGC* 248; to René Hague, 9–15 July 1973. DJ in conversation with Tony Stoneburner, written record 5 May 1966; letter draft frag. n.d.; DJ in 1964 to Solange Dayras, interviewed September 1989.

21 DJ quoted by E.C. Hodgkin, 'Some Memories of David Jones', typescript.

22 Letter frag. n.d.

23 DJ to Blissett, p. 64; DJ interviewed by Peter Orr, 1972; to René Hague, 15 July 1973; to Bernard Bergonzi, 11 November 1965; to Janet Carver, 5 July 1972; to René Hague, 9–15 July 1973.

24 To Harman Grisewood, 12 December 1966.

25 To Mr [Thomas] Whitaker draft, 1970; DJ in conversation with author, 4 June 1971; DJ to Blissett, p. 66.

26 To Tony Stoneburner, 30 July 1969; to Miss [Jane] Carver, 5 July 1972.

27 To Sister Mary Ursula, draft, n.d.

28 To Tom Burns, 14 September–5 October 1940; *IP* 176–7.

29 John Ellis, *Eye-Deep in Hell: Trench Warfare in World War I* (Baltimore: Johns Hopkins University, 1976), p. 52. I am also indebted elsewhere and in many ways to this marvellous book.

30 To Harman Grisewood, 21 May 1940.

31 Record made by E. C. Hodgkin immediately after his conversation with DJ in hospital in 1970; to Harman Grisewood 2 October 1964.

32 DJ in conversation with author, 4 June 1971; DJ to Blissett, p. 74.

33 To David Blamires, 6 November 1966; MS draft frag. n.d.

34 DJ annotation to Munby, p. 25.

35 *DGC* 252.

CHAPTER 7

MOSTLY BOIS GRENIER

The Battle of Passchendaele would continue disastrously for the next four months, but the 15th Battalion, which had fought hard and suffered great losses, would not rejoin it. In August and September in reserve billets at Proven, Leipsig Farm and Langemark, they were subject to training in musketry and bayonet-fighting and underwent extended order drill, route marches, specialist training, and gas drill. Jones detested all this but most hated bayonet-practice, which was led by instructing sergeants demanding that they pretend ferocity, shout obscenely, and not spare the enemy's eyes and genitals – it was for him 'revolting'. He later wrote, 'after you've been in a fairly rough house, to be taught how to do the stuff is ridiculous nonsense: you must hate the enemy, and so on'. In all his time in thetrenches he would never see anyone bayoneted.[1]

64. 'Breilen Aug 18, 1917, N.W. of Ypres Mark I or Mark IV Tank?'

While they were in reserve, an enemy aeroplane dropped a bomb among the bivouacs, killing one, wounding ten. Jones made three sketches of the ruins of Breilen, one with a British tank in the middle distance and heavy artillery shells upright in the foreground. (fig. 64).

The weeks of training and marching and drill were hateful to all of them, but the battalion was now too weak for battle, so it was finally sent, on the 25 September, to the unusually quiet Bois Grenier sector. They entered the front line just as a Welsh battalion on their right conducted a raid. In retaliation, Jones's battalion suffered heavy trench-mortar fire the next day and artillery fire at night. Then things became quiet, except for 2 October, when they were shelled all day. Because the battalion was thinly spread – as was the entire 38th Division, holding the line from Armentières to Laventie – tours of duty in the coming weeks excluded periods in divisional reserve.

At this time he was granted his second leave, to begin on 4 October in the week his parents were moving house. Disinclined to spend his leave helping with unpacking and advising on the placement of furniture and the hanging the family pictures, he asked for a postponement, vaguely explaining to the incredulous adjutant that there was trouble at home which made being there inconvenient. The officer remarked that this was a new twist on the common request for early leave because of 'trouble at home'. He consulted the orderly-room sergeant and, reminding Jones that he might not live to take a postponed leave, arranged a swap with another man so that Jones could go on the 14th.[2]

Leave lasted ten days, including travel-time. On 15 October, when he arrived at Victoria Station, he was, as usual, crawling with body lice. He went straight to his parents' new semi-detached house, called Hillcrest, at 115 Howson Road in Brockley. Without stopping, he went through the main door at the side of the house and up the stairs to the bathroom, removed his uniform and underclothes, and threw them out of the window. In a recent letter, his mother had insisted that he discard his clothing in this way. (Although leaves were unannounced, his mother had known he was returning – she always did, his father told him and, laughing, said, 'Your mother isn't Welsh but she's a bit of a witch.') Looking out of the window, he saw his sister approaching the pile of lousy clothing and shouted, 'FOR CHRIST SAKE, LEAVE THE FUCKING THINGS ALONE.' The profanity astonished her – such language had never been heard in the Jones home. Himself appalled, he watched his language at home from now on. After bathing, he put on his civilian clothes, which no longer fit. In a photograph taken during this leave, the cuffs of his trousers are three inches above the tops of his shoes.

Again he felt uneasy 'owing', he wrote, 'to the utter impossibility of answering the question "What's it really like out there?"' When asked about 'our gallant allies the French', he replied, 'Better the Fourth Bavarian for backup than the bloody Frogs!' – the general impression among British infantry being that the French were poor soldiers. The antipathy was, he knew, reciprocal – the French regarding the British as drunkards and/or as just having come from French girls.[3]

His curtness was more expressive of pique, however, than irritation with the French, whom he actually liked. After the assault on Pilckem Ridge, he and his companions had exchanged with French infantry bully beef and other rations for long French loaves. In the sector north of Ypres, the French had held the line to their immediate left and had several times been neighbours to D Company, whose members were always glad to trade for their 'real bread'. Jones had noticed 'how different all sorts of things' were in the French trenches, where they used wattled pens to form gabions packed with earth, which worked 'exactly like . . . defences' he had 'seen in early photographs of the Crimean War'. These French infantry were bearded and elderly, members of a militia corps. Insisting on silence, lest the enemy hear and send over trench-mortar shells, they used to shush the noisy young Cockneys, who would jeer, 'Got the wind up proper, Old 'un. Why, there's a tidy width of Canal between Jerry an' us.' Jones admired the 'splendid work' of the French on roads and reinforcing of trenches, especially communication trenches, with beautiful wattled revetments, the look of which he loved. On one occasion, he overheard a French lieutenant 'mothering' (as he would remember) 'his battered, overloaded, and exhausted men with heartening words that began *Mes enfants*'. For Jones it was an epiphany of the root-meaning of 'infantry', which would influence the imagery of his war epic, whose dedication is shared by 'THE BEARDED INFANTRY' of France of this sector north of Ypres.[4]

Sometime 'during the war' – it may have been while returning from this leave – he became desperately seasick. He had not been seasick on previous crossings and would not be during subsequent voyages, but now, he would remember, the waves were 'perpendicular in ascent and descent'. He was too ill to fear or to care whether he lived or died, too ill even to wish to die. Over three decades later, he would remember this experience when writing about a medieval ship struggling under the 'green arching darks' of great 'tilted heavers' whose 'imménser hovers dark-ápse her' (A 140) – 'hovers' referring to 'the great waves meeting over the . . . vessel'.[5]

He was happy to be in trenches at Bois Grenier. The land was flat, the trenches old, and communication trenches, he thought, 'quite beautiful' with flowering Morning Glory and other convolvuli tangling over revetment frames. (One of the ruined farms in the area was said to be the setting of the early Bruce Bairnsfather cartoon captioned, 'We are billeted in a farm'.) Part of the front line was a ruined monastery. A little boy, blowing a little horn to announce his presence, came regularly to the road at the entrance to the communication trenches selling French newspapers. The battalion would remain here through most of the autumn of 1917 and return in January and February 1918. It was the quietest front Jones experienced, with opposing trenches 300 yards apart. He 'had quite a nice time' here.[6]

Again he was attached to the intelligence officer at Battalion Headquarters with whom, as he put it, he used to 'mooch about a bit at night' in no man's land making sketch-maps of enemy saps and trenches. He found these maps 'awful things to make' because he kept 'putting things in the wrong place' and he later said that he 'was not much use' at making them. In self-criticism he may have exaggerated;

if his map-making was not valued, he would hardly have been required to do it on and off for three years. He also drew finished maps and wrote reports. He would commemorate himself as military cartographer in a fictional character temporarily assigned to head-quarters and named 'Private W. Map' (IP 127). According to the Welsh colloquial practice of identifying a person by his occupation, 'Walter Map' could identify someone named Walter David Jones who made maps.*[7]

Mapping no man's land and his battalion sector since early 1916 intensified his spatial imagination in ways that would influence his art. Throughout his life his imagination would have a decade-long incubation period – important experiences taking approximately that long to gestate in his subconscious and then emerge in his painting or poetry. His visual art of a decade later, and increasingly from then on, would be characterised by irregular areas of colour, wandering lines and distorted perspective that give them striking affinity with maps. He had been fascinated with the trench-mazes of the Ploegsteert and Boesinghe sectors but also felt considerable affinity for the common, single wavering line more typical of British defences, a line (such as he would draw 'with the point') which he would later think differentiated the British imagination from that of other nations. It would certainly differentiate his imagination from those of other visual artists and writers (British or not) except Joyce in *Finnegans Wake*. In Jones's poetry after *In Parenthesis*, the narrative and rhetorical 'lines' would waver freely to chart the geography of his imaginative engagement with historical culture. His interest in maps had not begun with the war and would not end with it. As a young history buff, he had been fasci-nated by them and he later sought them out in history books. He would acquire them to aid his writing, sometimes drawing copies of them. In 1943 he commented, 'Strange how any map is so convincing & real & how one can never make up a map – well, not strange at all

---

* In the poem, moreover, '79 Map' has the number of '79 Jones'. The fictional character also commemorates the twelfth-century Welshman Walter Map who was attached to Henry II's court, a sort of headquarters.

really, because it is reality'.[8] He would also say of a drawing or painting, 'it is reality'.

Shells fell occasionally at Bois Grenier, but, after the mechanised inferno of the Ypres Salient, life in this sector was a pastoral idyll. He was particularly fortunate to be stationed at headquarters, which was a cottage hidden from hostile view by an overgrown hedge. Water was the primary enemy here, and he sometimes worked on fatigues to grade trenches so it could drain away. Whenever a trench was blown in by a shell, neighbouring trenches flooded. In heavy rain, all trenches flooded. Even in the best weather, some trenches remained running drains through which men could move but not rest or build dugouts.

He had the leisure to sketch in some detail the hamlet of Elverdinghe (fig. 65), now a military supply depot, on 26 October.

He would remember the sector as 'uncannily quiet'. (The most common battalion diary-entry is 'very quiet day'.) Lulled into a sense of security and because he was sleeping alone in a little dugout in the support line, he ignored standing orders not to remove boots at

65. 'Elverdinghe. NW of Ypres 21.9.17'

night in forward or support trenches. The quiet continued until the night of 25 October 1917. He would remember being 'snug in this cubby-hole wrapped in a complex of blankets – my boots off & feeling pretty good' as he fell asleep only to be awakened by 'a hurricane of enemy shelling' – the worst barrage he had experienced. His little dugout 'shook with the vibrations of near H. E. bursts'. Although 'only half awake and very bewildered', he could also distinguish low bursts of medium shrapnel, long-distance 'nine-fives', and twelve-inch shells trundling far over the support line. A barrage in such depth usually heralded an attack. Quickly he put on his left boot but could not find the other. He lit the stub-end of a candle, but the shaking of the earth extinguished it. He could not run safely through the trenches with one foot bare. In what seemed an endless nightmare, he felt frantically for the other boot, eventually finding it tangled in his equipment. After putting it on, he emerged onto the duckboards. In the misty pre-dawn half-light, the violence of fire 'from every

66. Equipment

conceivable calibre of gun' had worsened. He and the others in the trench presumed that the forward companies had been over-run. Major Edwards was standing on the fire-step, his 'handsome, stern, anxious face' peering into the fog. Before long, the 'tornado of violence' ended. There was no crackle of rifle fire, so no assault. Not knowing that the shelling was retaliation for a raid carried out that night by a Welsh battalion on their right, Jones supposed it to be a try-out for some future offensive. Never again would he disobey standing orders to keep boots on while in the trenches.[9]

Whenever enemy shelling increased in this sector, it was often in retaliation for raids – mostly carried out by Australians holding the line to the left. They were avid about raids, which were unpopular with Jones and his companions, who considered them 'dishonest – like burglary' – and pointless. The Australians would bring back great numbers of prisoners and also, to Jones's horror, decapitated heads. But Australian barbarism had at least one positive consequence. Jones had seen British privates undergoing 'field punishment number one', known as 'crucifixion' – sergeant-majors would order men tied for days to the rim of a limber wheel by wrists and ankles, with arms extended. (He once assumed the position for a short while to see how it felt and found it very uncomfortable.) He was glad to hear that an Australian, upon seeing a private tied to the wheel for two days running, sought out the sergeant-major, and, by threatening his life, stopped the punishment.[10] Threats by Australians were taken seriously.

In November, Jones's battalion was twice assigned to instruct a Portuguese unit – and ordered, the second time, not to refer to these 'gallant allies' as the 'Pork & beans' or the 'bloody geese'. On the night of the 28th, Jones was assigned to help wire a reserve trench. The fatigue party consisted of a young lieutenant, a Welsh sergeant, 6 other privates, and 30 Portuguese. They arrived at their destination to find the trench merely a shallow indentation marked by engineers with white tape. When shells began falling behind them, the Portuguese scrambled into a ditch by the side of a road and refused to budge. Enraged, the sergeant threatened to shoot them but they understood neither Welsh nor English. The others put out some wire and tried to deepen the hollow between the tapes. As dawn approached, the young lieutenant was almost in tears because it was his duty upon returning to report their mission accomplished. The Portuguese were not cowards, Jones realised, who knew their reputation as knife-fighters; they were peasants unsuited to 'an essentially Industrial type of war'. He had noticed that, in general, conscripts from rural areas were more bewildered and lost than those from cities. The Portuguese were not only 'useless under shell-fire', he later remembered, but also 'caused much difficulty' because of sanitary habits uncongenial to the British.[11]

Upon returning from convalescent leave in the autumn of the previous year, he had acquired a khaki-covered Reeves sketchbook in which he continued to make drawings, many while with the Survey, fewer after returning to his unit. He sketched his boots, his equipment hanging on a peg (fig. 66), the captured howitzer and machine-gun (ch. 6, figs. 62, 63), and buildings torn open by artillery. Before the Somme, men had been the primary subject of his sketches, some of them so vivid as to be recognizably portraits; now he seldom drew men and usually perfunctorily. Only 14 of these 41 sketches are

67. '(probably
Elverdinghe church)
Flanders 1917'

of soldiers. The shift away from the human figure to landscapes and still-life reflects emotional withdrawal from his companions to objects that could not, by being killed or maimed, cause suffering. (To the end of his life, he later said, visual images of 'wounded men' haunted his memory.) Most of these drawings are of ruined buildings: one of a row of smashed houses, another of a ruined nave and tower of *'probably* Elverdinghe church 1917' (fig. 67). Psychologically, these ruins displace men and serve as their symbolic counterparts. This is suggested by the language he uses to describe ruins, such as a church 'cut in a kind of cross-section by a shell-burst & all the construction showing like bones laid bare'. It was now that he realised he liked 'things shorn & a bit maimed'. Only such things were true to the human condition. The dead rats he drew (ch. 6, fig. 56) seem also to have something of this symbolically displaced humanity.[12]

Jones still carried in his knapsack one of his two poetry anthologies. In his early months at the front, he had found that reading poetry aroused disdain in his Cockney companions, who considered it an interest of sissies. There was also a semi-official belief that the cultivation of sensitivity was bad for morale because it could only heighten awareness of what Jones later called 'the futilities, stupidities and bestialities' of warfare. Despite this and the weight a book added to his pack, he continued reading poetry. Now, however, he was finding it increasingly difficult to enjoy because of

> the feeling that the writers and compilers of most works were remote from us and our particular realities. . . . that they knew no calamity comparable to what we knew; that they wrote of death and hurts and despair in highfalutin' terms, without our close-up, day by day contact with such things, and consequently 'literature' rather slid away into that lost world of comfort and safety and illusion that we felt we had finished with, probably for ever. The great writers became almost as remote from us as were those friends and relatives we tried so hard to keep contact with in our letters home – always knowing

that our secret new world was hidden from them. . . .we were so impressed with being the first men of our race to face real war under modern conditions that we tended, inside ourselves, to be impatient of the writings and words of those who had not shared our trials.

He would later decide that feelings of diminished connection with the literary-historic past 'were largely unreal and exaggerated'.[13] To some degree, *In Parenthesis* would effect a rapprochement with literary tradition, many of the allusions in his war epic being to poems in the anthologies he was reading.* Yet *In Parenthesis* is unlike that poetry, and much of the literature it alludes to predates the verse canonised by English anthologies.

His sense of distance from the literary past is reflected in his fourth drawing made for publication in *The Graphic*, probably in mid-November. Reproduced murkily (fig. 68) in the 8 December issue, it is remarkable in several respects. Accompanying it is the caption 'The Wrack of War by Private W. David Jones', and the words of Mark Antony's funeral oration in *Julius Caesar*: 'O judgment! thou art fled to brutish beasts, / And men have lost their reason' (III, ii, 104–5). Like Adam and Eve exiting paradise, a couple departs the picture frame. The man in the lead, wearing laurels and carrying a staff and book, represents the Liberal Arts. The woman carrying a lyre and representing music has removed her laurel crown. Two leopards enter behind them ostensibly to take their place. In the background are the ruins of a church, based on his sketch of '*probably*' Elverdinghe church near Ypres (fig. 67). Further back are factory chimney-stacks spewing black smoke. Clearly the ruined church has gone the way of humane culture, and

---

* Poems alluded to in *In Parenthesis* from Arthur Quiller-Couch's *Oxford Book of English Verse* or Palgrave's *Golden Treasury with Additional Poems* (1912) are: Dunbar's 'Lament for the Makers', Wyatt's 'They flee from me', the folk song 'Barbara Allen', Milton's 'Hymn on the Morning of Christ's Nativity', Shirley's 'Death the Leveller', Coleridge's 'The Rime of the Ancient Mariner' and 'Christabel', Southey's 'After Blenheim', and Wolfe's 'The Burial of Sir John Moore'.

68. The Wrack of War,
The Graphic,
8 December 1917

the industrial smoke-stacks are meant to resonate symbolically with brutishness, indicating that if war is loss of rational culture, so is modern industrialisation. The enemy here is not Germany but dehumanising civilisational change. The allegory fails, however, because the lovely leopards resist the negative significance assigned them by the quotation from Shakespeare. They seem, rather, to join their human counterparts in sadly departing the uncongenial wasteland as if both couples were seeking, two by two, an ark to deliver them. This picture is an early indication of Jones's antipathy to industrialisation, which reflects his reading of Ruskin and Morris and would strengthen his friendship with Eric Gill and influence Jones's poetry.

In the Bois Grenier sector in the spring of 1917, he had become friendly for the first time in his life with a Catholic, a chaplain named Daniel Hughes SJ, called by the men 'the padre'. Assigned to the brigade but stationed with a solidly Methodist Welsh battalion, he visited the London Welsh for company, though even here he scandalised some by drinking whisky with the men. Jones would remember him as 'a hell of a nice chap, . . . a remarkable man and of great bravery'. (Catholic chaplains were generally well liked because they ignored pressure by military authorities to stay out of the combat zone, unlike Anglican chaplains, who were allowed no further forward than Brigade Headquarters.) Hughes insisted on administering the sacraments to the dying and had won the Military Cross for risking his life doing it. The impression made on Jones by his glimpse of the Mass some months before moved him to speak to Hughes about the Catholic Church, to which he increasingly felt drawn. Hughes lent him St Francis de Sales's *The Introduction to the Devout Life*, a spiritual classic intended for lay people. It was the first religious book by a Catholic that Jones read.[14]

To Jones the destruction and boredom of war typified an emptiness in life, for which, he increasingly felt, the only antidote was meaning of the sort he had glimpsed in the Mass north of Ypres. The virtues occasioned by war – the heroism, the patience, the love between soldiers – and the general goodness of the men implied, he thought, a significance that ultimately could only be spiritual. The meaning of virtue in ordinary people is precisely what Francis de Sales emphasises in his *Introduction to the Devout Life*. Anglican Christianity had become, for Jones, a matter of dead routine, a convention to which he subscribed rather than a vital experience and an awareness. 'There was something pretty unlovable about those official "church parades"', he would remember, 'very Erastian' (subordinate to the state) 'and totally devoid of the sacramental'. As the war tested the efficacy of the forms and resources of Anglican and nonconformist Christianity, many sensitive men became sceptics and agnostics, but his way of shedding superficial Christianity was conversion to something deeper. His conversion was a reaffirmation of his childhood faith but also a discovery of something theologically richer and with historic claims and dimensions that the Church of England lacked. He thought now that he would become a Roman Catholic and would later say that he was 'inside, a Catholic' from this time.[15]

Poulter was also drawn to Catholicism through Hughes. In Jones's dugout, he and Jones talked about their new shared interest, sometimes while sharing another kind of spiritual sustenance, 'whisky kindly' but unknowingly 'provided by the R.S.M' through Poulter. Jones's friend entered the Catholic Church during the war, as did 'a lot' of others influenced by Hughes, but Jones hesitated. Given a chance, he usually procrastinated, and this was a big decision, one which, he knew, would greatly upset his parents. He did not, moreover, find Catholics generally as appealing as Hughes. To his 'discomfort', as he later said, a number of Irishmen in his battalion, though identified as practising Catholics by their use of the rosary, were characterised by 'crude, revolting, unchristian discourtesy'.[16]

On 30 November the battalion moved three miles north to Erquinghem, a violent sector where heavy artillery fell on them almost daily. On 11 December the bombardment was so intense that they retreated from the forward trench. The enemy advanced, entered the trench under cover of the barrage and, finding it empty, retired. For Christmas 1917 the battalion was in reserve in the village of Erquinghem. It was Jones's third Christmas in France, celebrated with Poulter and other companions. He would remember it as 'almost the only' Christmas of his adult life that he 'really enjoyed'.[17]

In November, he had finished a drawing together with a short pseudo-medieval allegory in the style of William Morris's late prose romances. Entitling both the drawing and writing *The Quest*, he had sent them home for his father to print as a New Year's card, a three-page string-bound pamphlet. In the drawing on the cover (fig. 69), an aspiring knight and bare-shouldered damsel are once again idealisations of himself and Elsie Hancock, very much as they appear in *Lancelot and Guenevere* (ch. 5, fig. 44). Behind the knight is a harp-carrying bard, who also resembles Jones. Also present is a helmeted knight and a monkish scholar. Here in its entirety, is the writing accompanying the picture:

69. The Quest, *New Year 1918*

The Quest

Now, a very great while ago there set out upon a quest a certain company of people, among the which were a Knight, a Lady, a Minstrel, and a Man of Letters. Now, the name or ancestry of the Knight no man knew, for he bore not upon his shield the emblazonry of his sires, but a red heart all aflame, because his heart did ever burn within him. And the Lady was most desirous fair, insomuch that many there were whose hearts were nigh unto breaking because of her. The Minstrel was exceeding skilled upon his instrument, and sang most wondrous pretty lays, enchanting all who heard him. And, lastly, the Scholar was surpassing well learned in all the ancient lore, and did instruct others therein.

The quest that they did follow after was yclept 'The Quest of the Castle called Heart's Desire'.

So they travelled in many lands. Oft-times they were passing weary and forlorn; oft they did utterly despair. Now, it chanced upon a certain day, that as they made their journey they came upon a lonesome mountain track, thorn-grown and wild; huge boulders, cruelly rough, encumbered all their path, and it was hard going.

But when they got them to the topmost crag, there lay before their marvelling eyes a wondrous sight and passing pleasant, – a Castle bathed in golden light, fairly proportioned, girt with matchless towers.

Now, when they that were come did see this thing, they wept for very joy; for, 'Behold', said they, 'surely this is none other than the stronghold of our dreams'.

He who was lord, and kept the place, was a mighty lord withal; yet held he neither slave, serf, nor unwilling vassal, and they that did pour forth the wine at his board were esteemed as great as they that drank thereof. And they that did hew wood and did work among the pots, – these, also, were not called 'mean', 'knave', or 'churl', as is the custom in the haunts of proud and mighty men. And because that great lord ruled with equity, therefore was this thing possible!

When the eyes of the company that came to seek were become dazed at the sight so fair, and the wonder of it, they looked for to find a way whereby they might by some means get them to the Castle gate; for even yet it was far off. And when they looked their hearts did sink with fear; for betwixt them and the place of their desire lay a weary stretch of broken march-land, choked with weeds, and haunted of foul beasts; and yet again behold, a fearsome mere, broad, unspanned by bridge, and without ford. In truth, there was a barge, but it lay in moorings on the farther side.

And whilst they stood and wondered, very dolorous, one rose up among them, and spake on this wise: 'Hearken, all ye whose hearts be burning with the unquenchable flame of unfulfilled desire, – hearken ye to me!'

Now spake he to the young Knight: 'Sir Knight, the men of valour in yonder wondrous hall, when they make them wars, war not but for the cause of liberty. Thou, therefore, when thou liftest high thy battle-blade, strike not but to make men free. And if a great prince shall say to thee, 'Sir, fight thou for me, and for my fair province, for surely thy reward shall be great', thou shall cry scorn upon him and upon his province; for he speaketh a vain thing, and after the manner of princes. But if one grey-headed shall cry unto thee, saying, 'Fair Sir, they have taken from me the only ox that I had, and despoiled me of mine only acre', then shalt thou straightway raise thy sword for him, – yea though it meaneth a right bloody affray. Thou shalt e'en esteem thy life well hazarded in such a cause.'

Then unto the Lady he spake. 'In that most perfect isle, the maidens, when they love, love only to keep their lovers pure. O thou, whose beauty doth destroy the hearts of men, when thou art filled with the wild emotion of desire, see that thou use thy matchless love to help thy lover live the better.'

Then spake he thus to the Bard: 'The peerless skalds who sing the saga of the greatness of yon king, tune their harp-strings ever to the noblest lays; likewise thou, when thou playest, cause thine instrument to fire the hearts of men with strong and blameless zeal.'

Then turned he to the Scholar and said: 'Across the dread marchland there dwell begowned seers, who seek only to learn and teach that which is pure and faultless true. Do thou likewise, that black ignorance and the teaching that doth corrupt may cease through the land.'

'Weep not, ye desirous ones, weep not because ye cannot yet attain unto the land of your fond hopes. Go ye, – hie ye back each to your separate place, and do these things. And upon a day the mighty king, who rules in equity o'er his domains, shall, with his own strong hand, guide you through the uncharted tracks; shall lead you o'er the broken marchland; shall steer you in his royal barge across the mere's broad expanse, even to the gates of His Own Palace, and lead you in! Then shall ye have in full your dear hearts' pure desire. Foreasmuch as ye have come upon this worthy quest, therefore have ye seen what ye have seen. For, of a truth, 'Where is no vision, surely the inhabitants shall wholly perish.'

Now, this is the story of 'The Quest of the Castle called Heart's Desire'. He that knoweth the interpretation thereof, let him interpret.

The Trenches, France,
November, 1917

This, Jones's first purely fictional writing, is implicitly autobiographical. It reflects irritation at the inequities of military rank and the class system, and reveals an affinity with Morris-like socialism. He was a soldier, like the Knight, and the injunction to the Knight (by, perhaps, the voice of conscience) implies an altruistic belief in the Allied cause, made explicit in the pamphlet's prefatory greeting: 'May the coming year bring Confidence and Hope to all such as seek to uphold the cause of Emancipation and Liberty and to shatter the cult of Militarism and Aggression.' As an avid reader since early adolescence, he had been something of a 'Man of Letters'. Now (writing this allegory) he was a Minstrel/Bard, albeit somewhat immature and extremely idealistic. And in Elsie he had his Lady, who could only make him 'pure' and 'better'. The allegory is fundamentally moral and religious, of course, with God as the lord of the castle (heaven) and guarantor of chivalric values.* In January 1918 his battalion returned to Bois Grenier, where conditions had worsened. In anticipation of a

---

* Jones would never waver from the basic conviction behind this allegory. Two decades later, in a response to his friend Herbert Read's contention, in *Poetry and Anarchy*, that freedom in politics is the same as freedom in art and can lead to utopian political anarchy, Jones would reply that while 'an art-work is a similitude to the Kingdom of God', life is distinct from art, and we ought to keep our 'vanishing points outside Time.' *Tablet* (16 July 1938), p. 77.

major German offensive, the High Command ordered the entire division to spend the next four months strengthening the line in depth. This meant increased fatigues: digging trenches, filling and stacking sandbags, assembling revetments, laying barbed wire, and constructing concrete defences as far back as the river Lys, two miles away.

The Bois Grenier sector was now as familiar to him as the Richebourg sector had been in 1916. It was still a friendly place compared to the desolate area north of Ypres. One quiet night, he and Poulter discussed the prospects that the Bois Grenier sector would offer to tourist agencies when peace came. He later remembered,

> we went into glowing details & wondered if the unexploded projectile lying near us would go up under a bright holiday maker & how girls in muslin frocks would stand & be photographed on our parapets. I recall feeling very angry about this, like you do if you think of strangers ever occupying a house or garden you live in & love. There was a great sense of possessiveness among us. It was always 'our trenches' 'our dugouts' – *we* knew exactly the kind of shell *he* was likely to put on . . . *we* knew the best way across the open to where the big crater was, where the good water was. Some twist of traverse in a disused trench-system had for us something of the quality of the secret places lovers know.[18]

He was acutely sensitive to place and now especially this place.

Rain, sleet and snow fell throughout January and February. On 14 January 1918 the entire 38th Division left the sector for the last time, and he felt considerable regret. They marched 14 miles west to Le Sant near Merville. Rain fell heavily. The farm buildings where they billeted were soon surrounded by water. They could move outside only by wading. He would remember, 'it was also, at least part of the time, *appallingly* cold'.[19] Mercifully, the flooding precluded drill and training.

Here orders came that greatly distressed him. Depleted by casualties, the number of battalions in the brigade was to be reduced from four to three in order to bring battalions up to full strength. The 15th Battalion was to be abolished, its companies going intact to other battalions in the brigade. As one of the few surviving members to arrive with the battalion in France, he, more than most, dreaded the end of 'cap-badge loyalty', an aspect of the fellowship that made military life endurable. On 6 February, the battalion was officially disbanded in a funerary ceremony for which Colonel Bell returned especially to deliver a eulogy. The actual dispersal of the companies of the battalion took place in mid-February – Jones going with D Company into the line near Armentières with the 13th Battalion.

In his copy of an account of the war during this period, he would place a large, endorsing X in the margin beside the following passage: 'A feature of the stationary warfare of these latter months . . . was the system of Artillery "Crashes", or salvos, which was employed by both sides; these crashes were probably accountable for far more casualties than any systematic bombardment in such warfare, for they came whenever and wherever least expected.'[20] These crashes made life in the line especially nerve-wracking. All at once and suddenly, noisy death and maiming fell all along the forward and support lines and then almost immediately ceased, leaving a treacherous quiet.

In fact, an important casualty of these crashes especially but also of other artillery fire was quiet itself, which is the sensory basis of psychological equanimity. Except while on leave, in divisional reserve, and when with the Survey, he had experienced some degree of enemy shelling almost daily and an extensive bombardment, on average, twice a week for the past three years. Over this time but especially now, quiet became a horribly pregnant time-between. He would later suffer two nervous breakdowns and decades of depression, which have, at the very least, contributing causes in experience of years of artillery fire culminating with these 'crashes' and their consequently disquieting hiatuses.

From his first arrival in the trenches through the autumn of 1916, he had been deeply, irrationally convinced that he would survive the war. As time passed and so many of his companions were killed, he began to doubt that he would survive. Now he felt that probably he would not – the odds were against it. 'There was no let-up at all for the infantry', he later remembered. 'It was continuous – I felt the sands running out. . . . When I went out to France I was a first-class shot. In my last year I was rated third-class. You just went off, or perhaps you didn't care any longer.' Since the Somme, life in the trenches had elicited 'a feeling akin to indifference, tedium'.[21]

He was, of course, suffering from some degree of shell-shock, an ill-named ailment since it is not shock, though its cause is shellfire. Forty years later it would be called 'War Neurosis' and, later still, post-traumatic stress syndrome. Its symptom is unbearable fear. Cases were either hysteric or neurasthenic. The hysteric is the stereotype: a man suddenly becomes a frightened child, crying, clinging to his nearest companion, pleading not to be left alone. Jones witnessed such behaviour (see *IP* 153). Far more common, however, was the neurasthenic, which included many, perhaps most, combatants. Their anxiety gradually increased, often resulting in a breakdown, sometimes delayed, so that a man going on leave might collapse upon reaching Victoria Station. But delays might extend to six months or longer. Paradoxically, the very conditions to which fear was a response could postpone its manifestation. In most, being actually under fire evoked resilience and stiffened resolve. Neurasthenic symptoms were also masked by dullness and tedium. Jones was not treated for shell-shock during the war; after the Somme, very few neurasthenic cases were even diagnosed. Those afflicted with the condition might suffer nervous breakdowns years later or endure unclimactic, lingering neurosis, which kept a great many ex-servicemen from leading conventionally happy or productive lives. They would withdraw from social involvement, communal activity, or personal commitment – many would find human intimacy impossible. A decade after the war (before the Great Depression), when they might have been expected to be well established in careers, ex-servicemen would constitute 80 per cent of the unemployed. In some but not all respects, Jones would be one of these. His time under fire in the trenches may not be the sole cause of later unhappiness but it was sufficient cause. For the last three of his first 22 years, his psyche had been repeatedly, brutally assaulted.

Physical good health was endemic in the trenches, where the common cold was almost unknown, and, physically, the years at the front were his healthiest, but on a misty cold day in mid-February, he began to feel sharp shooting pains in his shins and came down with a high fever – it felt to him like 'the worst imaginable type of flu'. It was trench fever, what doctors called 'Pyrexia, Unknown Origin', a disease related to typhus and spread by lice. He would later remember that, 'curiously enough' he became ill *almost on the day* the London Welsh were disbanded', an event he had so dreaded that, he speculated, 'perhaps that's why I suddenly got trench-fever!' He was excused all duty and sent to divisional reserve, his fever remaining at 105 degrees for several days. His neck and face swelled and the surface of his tongue turned green. It was a severe case, involving 'disorderly action of the heart'. He was evacuated to Base Hospital, where he nearly died, and from there to a hospital in north London. There he remained for three months and was visited by his family. With no known cure, the illness had to run its course. He completed his convalescence in nursing homes.[22]

His years of combat were now over. About them he later said, 'I'm not sure I killed anyone, though I ought to have done. What I didn't like was the Mills bomb, tossing it down into a German dugout, killing or maiming someone you couldn't see. It was horrible.' He added, 'On the other hand, shooting a chap, having taken aim at him with a Lee Enfield rifle, seems quite a respectable thing to do.'[23]

On 21 March, a few days after his evacuation to England, the Germans began their last great offensive of the war, the Battle of Lys, which he followed in newspapers. As with the assault on Pilckem Ridge, he vicariously felt the ordeal of his former companions. He could hardly believe that the German advance had overrun in a single day what had taken the Allies months to capture. Places he had known well were now behind enemy lines: Laventie and Fleurbaix, overrun by 9 April, Armentières on the 10th, and by the end of the month,

70. Preliminary Sketch 'Captive Civilisation'

Estaires and Merville, and Bailleul, which had been 20 miles behind the Bois Grenier trenches. His admiration increased for Lloyd George as the only member of Cabinet not to panic. (Jones later imitated him: 'If you think we will lose, *we will not!*') Reading accounts of the fighting, he became convinced that trench fever, which had nearly killed him, saved his life. A friend at the front, possibly Poulter, wrote to him, 'You know when to go sick, don't you!'[24]

Before becoming ill, he had sent drawings to the Camberwell School of Arts Sketch Club, which had asked him to contribute to its first show since the start of the war. He did, and the exhibition was on while he was in hospital. His father brought him a clipping from the *South London Press* of 15 March 1918, which reports that Sergeant F. W. Medworth R.F.A. had sent 'some interesting sketches of life in the garrison' where he was posted since being wounded early in the war. The paper also commends work by Lance-Corporal H. F. W. Hawkins as 'of interest' because of 'the conditions under which they

71. Captive Civilisation and
the Black Knight of Prussia,
The Graphic, 13 July 1918

were executed'. Hawkins was still in a hospital in Bristol being treated
for debilitating wounds. 'Mr W. David Jones' gets the highest praise
of all for exhibiting 'some drawings excellent both in conception and
execution, one of which', *The Wrath* [sic] *of War*, 'was recently reproduced by the "Graphic"' (fig. 68).

While convalescing, he was asked by Hartrick for another picture
for *The Graphic*. Jones made a rough preliminary sketch of a bare-
backed brunette being rescued from a German knight by a white
knight plunging his sword into the German (fig. 70). He revised this
sketch for his fifth and final drawing for *The Graphic* (fig. 71). It appeared
in the issue of 13 July. According to the accompanying note, it depicts
'Civilisation bound by the Black Knight of Prussia, who is challenged
by another Knight, who represents the Allies'. Confronting the
swarthy, ugly Prussian, his crusader-opponent sports a halo, wears
on his tunic a Christian cross, and holds in his hand a sealed scroll
representing Law. He has interrupted the rape of Civilisation – who,

once again, resembles Elsie Hancock, more eroticised than ever with her clothing partially stripped away.

This is his only published war drawing that is unsigned and not attributed to him by name. If he requested anonymity because of reservations about its design, publishing only for the money (five guineas), this would be a rare lapse in a lifetime of uncompromising artistic integrity. Moreover, the design is good, with cross, swords, curves, diagonals and rectangles resonating interestingly. Probably, therefore, he was uncomfortable depicting a hateful enemy while feeling compelled to express indignation over the recent German advance, which had, he knew, killed and maimed many of his former comrades. The calamity apparently intensified his early conviction that Germany threatened western civilisation, a conviction the Germans had done a lot to encourage. They had attacked civilian populations. From the air, they had bombed London, Liverpool and Paris, slightly damaging Notre Dame. From U-boats they had shelled English ports and seaside resorts and had killed civilians at sea. They had been the first to use asphyxiating chlorine gas in contravention of international law and the first to use mustard gas.

As his admonition to the knight in *The Quest* indicates, Jones was susceptible to propagandistic use of the saviour myth. As he understood it, he and his companions were fighting to save France and Belgium and also western culture, whose values Germany was violating. The myth imprinted his imagination, the saviour-archetype having been, as it would remain, central to his religious faith; it, and the motif of the freedom fighter, would be a prominent feature of his later poetry. Without being conscious of it, in all his subsequent writing and visual art he would himself approximate the archetype of the saviour as an artist striving to preserve the vital roots of western culture.

In July 1918, he was home on sick-leave. Visiting his former teachers, he listened to Reginald Savage describe the lovely village of Bois Grenier, where he had lived before the war, which Jones knew only as a ruin.[25] After his sick-leave, he went to a military camp near Liverpool, where men from the front were subjected to rehabilitation by means of endless drill, button-polishing, cleaning of equipment. It was, he would remember, 'ghastly'.

NOTES TO CHAPTER 7

1   Bailley, 'The Front Line'; to Saunders Lewis, 27 April 1974.

2   *DGC* 234. The precise dates in this paragraph are as David Jones recalls them in an unnamed month in a letter to Harman Grisewood, 9 October 1971. Since he regularly remembers in letters events of the war on their anniversary dates, the month of his leave was probably that of the letter, and the dates mentioned were probably not invented. The approximate time of his second leave can be confirmed by process of elimination. A photo of him on leave shows bushes in full leaf. It is unlikely that he would have been granted leave less than a year since his prior leave, in October 1916, and Jones told Tony and Pat Stoneburner (6 June 1966) that he received this leave 'a year' after his convalescent leave.

3   Cissy Hyne to Tony Hyne, interviewed June 1985; DJ to Blissett, p. 134; to Harman Grisewood, 9 October 1971; to Valerie Wynne Williams, 6 August 1962; DJ in conversation with author, 4 June 1971.

4   To Saunders Lewis, 27 April 1974; to Mr Korda, draft, n.d.; to Harman Grisewood, 7 July 1971; to Tony Stoneburner, 12 March 1964; *IP* 41.

5   To Tony Stoneburner, 20 December 1964; DJ in conversation with Tony Stoneburner, written record 26 May 1969.

6   MS frag. n.d.: DJ in the margin of his copy of Munby, p. 29.

7   *DGC* 203; to Saunders Lewis, 27 April 1974; David Blamires, 'The Medieval Inspiration of David Jones', *David Jones: Eight Essays*, ed. Roland Mathias (Llandysul: Gomer Press, 1976), p. 18.

8   *DGC* 243; to Jim Ede, 27 March 1943.

9   To Saunders Lewis, 27 April 1974; DJ, *Word and Image* IV (London: National Book League, 1972), p. 50; DJ to Blissett, p. 140; MS frag. n.d.

10 DJ in conversation with author, 4 June 1971; cf. DJ to Blissett, p. 73.

11 To Harman Grisewood, 2 February 1973; to Herbert Read, unposted, 18 November 1967; *DGC* 244; annotation to Munby, p. 30.

12 To David Blamires, 9 July 1966; to Clarissa Churchill, 11 December 1939. The sketches referred to here are reproduced in *David Jones, A Fusilier at the Front*, selected by Anthony Hyne (Bridgend: Seren, 1995).

13 *Tablet*, 13 January 1940.

14 To M. Wilkinson, 30 July 1965; to Peter Levi, 29 January 1965; DJ interviewed by Jon Silkin, 1971; DJ to Blissett, p. 127; DJ's annotation to Munby, p. 21.

15 To Sister Mary Ursula, draft, n.d.; Blissett, recalling visits to DJ in June 1973.

16 To Harman Grisewood, 9 October 1971; David Poulter to author, 9 February 1990; David Poulter, interviewed 11 June 1990; 'A Soldier's Memories', 506.

17 To Saunders Lewis, 20 December 1971; to Tony Stoneburner, 8–9 January 1970.

18 DJ interviewed by Jon Silkin, 1971; letter frag. n.d.

19 Annotation to Munby, p. 31.

20 Munby, pp. 46-7.

21 DJ to Blissett, p. 122; *Manchester Guardian*, 17 February 1964; letter draft, frag. n.d.; to John Roberts of Ganymed Press n.d. [1961]; DJ to Blissett, p. 122; letter draft, frag. n.d.; MS frag. n.d.

22 Ellis, p. 52; DJ biographical note for the British Council n.d. [c.1971]; DJ MS frag. n.d.; Bailley, 'The Front Line'; to Saunders Lewis, April 1971; letter draft frag. n.d.; DJ in conversation with Tony Stoneburner, written record 19 June 1966.

23 DJ quoted by Bailley, 'The Front Line'.

24 To Catherine Ivainer, 13 March 1961; to Harman Grisewood, 22 March 1972; DJ MS frag. n.d.; to Meic Stephens, 27 February 1973; DJ in conversation with author, 9 September 1972; Bailley, 'The Front Line'; DJ in conversation with Tony Stoneburner, written record 9 June 1966.

25 DJ MS frag. n.d.

CHAPTER 8

IRELAND

In August, Jones was sent to Limerick, Ireland, to join the 3rd Battalion of the Royal Welch Fusiliers permanently stationed there and under the command of Lieutenant-Colonel McCartny-Filgate, a surname that delighted Jones.[1] A thriving centre in rich, rolling dairy land, Limerick had several tanneries, tobacco factories and plants for the production of condensed milk to supply the troops. There were four bacon factories, four cinemas, and each Wednesday a cattle and sheep market. Architecturally impressive, the town had a long eighteenth-century body with a medieval head to the north, on King's Island, where an eleventh-century castle guarded the Shannon.

Because of its strategic importance on the river and, for over half a century, at the junction of railway links, Limerick was a garrison town with four barracks. Jones was stationed at the largest, the New Barracks (now Sarsfield Barracks) at the southern end of town. Built in 1789 and housing battalions of the Oxfordshire and Buckinghamshire Light Infantry and the Royal Welch Fusiliers, it was a vast compound of limestone buildings behind high walls. Soldiers drilled and practised in the adjacent countryside and on a firing range two miles north in what was called the Island Field, just outside the medieval city walls and within sight of the Clare Mountains to the north-west.

Limerick was peaceful when he arrived. Though most towns-people supported Irish independence, they were friendly to the British and unsympathetic to the Volunteers, as the Irish rebels called them-selves. The town was home to the Munster Fusiliers and the towns-people benefited financially from separation pay earned by sons and husbands in the British Army in France. The local paper was full of news and editorials praising the Irish contribution to the war effort, and British soldiers wandered the town with impunity. Here, at a cost of seven pence a pint, Jones acquired a liking for Guinness.

If the townspeople were largely pro-British, he was entirely pro-Irish. He had long entertained romantic sentiments about the Irish Celts and, as his father did, favoured Irish independence. Before the war he had followed the slow movement through parliament of Asquith's proposal for limited home rule, with Ulster resisting all the way. He remembered the pre-war threat of rebellion by military units at Curragh, which had been ordered north to enforce home rule against the Ulster Volunteers. He had seen a placard on a newsagent's shop across from Camberwell Art School that read, 'Will Ulster Fight or is it a Great Game of Bluff?' Until now, all that had been eclipsed for him by the war, the Easter Rising having barely registered with soldiers at the front. But he had read a newspaper from home denouncing the wickedness of Irish rebels thinking to take advantage of Britain in her hour of need, and he had thought, 'If this bloody journalist had seen the Irish regiments in action & the casualties they sustained he had better have held his tongue.' When the papers reported talk of extending conscription to Ireland, Leslie Poulter had smiled and said, his steel-grey eyes glistening, 'Quite right, except that more Irishmen have freely enlisted in the British Army than from any given English county – bloody funny.' Jones was aware of the general Irish refusal that had frustrated extension of conscription. He fully realised that British war propaganda about freedom, the sanctity of small nations and their right to self-determination implicitly contradicted British rule of Ireland, a country that had claimed a right to independence long before some of the countries for whose freedom Britain was now ostensibly fighting.[2]

He had civilian contacts among the Protestant ascendancy in Limerick. His father knew a fervent Church of Ireland doctor named Lang, a medical missionary to the Catholic poor who gave free medical services in his surgery, preaching as he worked. Prompted by a letter from Jones's father, Lang had Jones to his house, which was upriver from Limerick and was, Jones thought, 'jolly nice'. Lang was 'a nice bloke' but a 'muscular' Christian with a 'sort of General Gordon thing about him' that Jones found uncongenial. He heard that Lang once hired a jaunting-car whose driver, to whom he was preaching, stopped and took the horse out of the shafts and left him stranded, and Lang stayed for hours in the vehicle preaching to passers-by. Jones used to hear the urchins in town sing a song containing the line, 'Dr. Lang's mother has a cook-shop in hell'.

Lang introduced him to his assistants the elderly Misses Gregg, sisters of the Protestant Archbishop of Armagh. 'Entirely English', they invited him to lunch and tea when off duty. He alarmed them by asking whether another soldier, a Catholic, could accompany him one day to tea. They seemed to think his 'Catholic buddy might have horns & a tail', and he found this odd, since they were surrounded by Catholics with whom they seemed on quite good terms. His Catholic friend was Francis Salkeld, whom he drew in August playing piano (fig. 72). Salkeld shared his enthusiasm for poetry and gave him for his birthday a copy of *Georgian Poetry 1913–1918*, inscribed in mock Middle English to 'Hys Palle'. Other soldier-friends whose portraits he sketched at this time were Ezra Davey, playing a violin, and Dewi Owen (fig. 73).[3] Release from the probability of losing friends to the carnage at the front had freed him to draw people again.

72. 'Francis Salkeld Limerick Aug 1918 by D. Jones'

73. 'Dewi Owen by David Jones. 1918. Limerick'

74. [on reverse] 'Eileen Gregg, Limerick, 1918'

Through the Misses Gregg, he met their niece Eileen Gregg, whom he found extremely attractive, 'a "stunner"'. While off duty, he and some of his friends from the 3rd Battalion used to visit her. A lovely young brunette, with a vivid personality, she gave him a photograph of herself (fig. 74). Another was taken with Salkeld standing behind her and Jones sitting beside her wearing her white tam-o'-shanter as a joke while she and Salkeld grin broadly. (The photo is not reproduced here because in it Jones's face is obscured by the sleeve of the photographer.) Jones also met and visited a young woman named Nanette MacFarlane, who gave him a copy of Edward Marsh's *Rupert Brooke: a memoir* (1918), and a photograph of herself and her sister, neither of them pretty. He was grateful to escape military routine occasionally and enjoy the company of young women.[4]

Because battle-weary troops were thought to need an infusion of the aggressive spirit, he was assigned to undergo assault training – as always, hateful to him. While practising storming enemy trenches, he badly sprained an ankle. A medical officer gave him a walking-stick and permission to use it. As he was hobbling across the parade-ground in barracks, a huge regimental sergeant-major, who had seen little combat, strode up and commanded, 'Put that stick down!' Jones explained that the M.O. had given him permission to use it. 'Put the bloody stick down', insisted the sergeant-major. 'No, sir, I have permission to use it.' After giving the order a third time and again being refused, he called over two soldiers, put Jones under arrest, and marched him to the guardroom to await court marshal. Notified, the medical officer did not object or intervene.

Jones spent three days and nights in the guardroom, which had a dirt floor and mattresses for six prisoners. In daytime a slanting ray of sunlight through a high, barred window penetrated the gloom, reminding him of Cruikshank's engravings of the Tower of London. He thought, 'Well, now I know what Byron was talking about in "The Prisoner of Chillon" – "dim with a dull imprisoned ray a sunbeam that had lost its way"'.[5]

Upon hearing that he was incarcerated, a friendly lieutenant named Evans, who had been on leave at the time of the arrest, visited him in the guardroom and expostulated, 'Jones, Jones, you can't be in this sort of mess.' When told what had happened, the lieutenant went to the sergeant-major and convinced him to reduce the charge from 'refusing three times to obey an order' to 'hesitation in obeying an order'. Removed from the cell, Jones was confined to barracks for two weeks. Afterwards, in town, the medical officer approached him and apologised for not backing him against the sergeant-major because, he said, 'we officers have to stick together'. Jones said nothing. The man's cowardice and the injustice rankled for a long time.[6]

Although Limerick was peaceful and its population generally pro-British, he was acutely conscious of some anti-British feeling. Members of rebel paramilitary units were regularly arrested and imprisoned in his barracks, and then the tension was palpable. At the main gate of the barracks, the mothers and sisters of the incarcerated Irish came up to the sentries and shouted in their faces, 'MURDERER!' (Their screeching and jeering had made one of his nights in the guardroom nightmarish.) When a sentry tried to shoo them away, they took the bayonet in their hands. It was hard to retain composure and 'very embarrassing', remembered Jones, who may, on occasion, have been one of these sentries. He associated the bravery of the women with that of unarmed Gordon facing his adversaries on the stairs at Khartoum. One night returning to barracks he saw a Cockney soldier holding his head, and Jones asked what was wrong, and the Cockney said he had been talking to an Irish girl on the street when a Catholic priest came up 'and knocked in my bloody face'.

In a small shop under the barracks wall where soldiers bought cigarettes and sweets, a copy of the 1916 Proclamation hung behind the proprietor and beside it a picture of Patrick Pearse over the words 'MURDERED BY THE ENGLISH'. Jones bought a copy of the Proclamation and hung it on the barrack-room wall, where the other soldiers read it with interest and respect.[7]

He sometimes stood guard at night on the banks of the rushing Shannon. In the dark he was afraid. How easy it would be, he thought, for a single push out of the darkness to tumble him, heavy in his greatcoat and equipment, into the fast-flowing water, which would weigh him down as it carried him away.[8]

Technically, he and his new companions were in reserve, subjected to parade-ground drill and training. While not involved in any active large-scale policing of the general population, they were ready to intervene if circumstances required, and he was 'beginning to get very worried'. He would remember, 'It's a jolly frightening thing to be in a place where there's an unseen enemy. I was entirely pro-Irish, but I was very worried because, I thought, if it comes to a real show-down I don't know what I will do. Probably I would be part of the crowd and do what I was told.'[9]

Each Sunday (accompanied by the regimental mascot, a large goat), his battalion paraded from New Barracks up O'Connell Street through Georgian Limerick into the medieval 'old town' to its twelfth-century cathedral. One Sunday as they marched, he saw an old woman trying to cross the street through a gap between platoons – something no civilian would have attempted in England. Jones saw the sergeant-major of his battalion elbow her back towards the pavement where she collapsed in the gutter. No one objected or went to her aid, including the well-bred officers passing her crumpled body. For the first time, he understood how serving in a hostile country affected the behaviour of soldiers. Fear made them cruel.[10]

His circumstance and that of his mates undoubtedly reminded him of first-century Roman soldiers subjugating the Celts in Britain. For the past three years he had read that he was fighting 'in defence of the Empire'. His serving now in a conquered, occupied part of the Empire would later bear literary fruit in the Roman poems of *The Sleeping Lord*. In one of them, 'The Dream of Private Clitus', a fictional Roman soldier recounts to a young conscript a first-century campaign against Germans in Teutoburg Forest (*SL* 15–23), just as now in Limerick Jones recounted to companions the assault on Mametz Wood.

Once, he was assigned to escort prisoners to Dublin. During the two-and-a-half-hour train ride to Westmorland Station, he gazed at the lush rolling countryside, thick with grazing cattle and, as they moved north, sheep and horses. The whitewashed stone houses resembled those of Wales. A ridge of bare hills appeared on his right, indistinguishable from Welsh hills. The Tipperary Mountains became visible in the east, reminding him that he had come 'a long way'. Deserted farmsteads and ruined cottages on the slightly rolling central plain recalled the Famine and expulsions by landlords. Although his visit to Dublin was brief, and despite the devastation at its centre caused by British shelling two years earlier, he liked the city.[11]

His months in Ireland impressed him. It was, as he said, 'a lovely country'. Years later he wrote: 'It made a fairly vivid impression especially the soft rain & the intense blueness of the distance & also the great beauty of young women very dirty in *red* skirts bare footed & in white shifts or blouses.'[12]

Once especially, he was affected by a young beauty. In the second week of November, he was taking part in elaborate day-long manoeuvres in the hills north of Cork. He and four companions got 'hopelessly lost' and agreed 'to bugger off and turn up at the end'. After a leisurely afternoon in the green countryside, the loitering fusiliers on a wet hill-road passed a barefoot young woman with loose, wind-blown red hair walking in the red light of the setting sun, driving before her a red-brown cow. 'A wild & almost savage figure' with 'the carriage of a princess', she wore a torn white shift and a homespun red wool skirt with a wide plum-coloured velvet hem that fell to just below her knees. Her legs, feet and arms were bare and 'her skin . . . of exceptional whiteness.' The reds of her hair, her skirt, its hem, and the cow burned in the lateral light. (Helen of Troy might have looked like that, he later thought.) He gazed after her, fearful that his mates would begin whistling and calling to her, but they, too, were spell-bound. She passed into a long low lime-whitened farm building, thatched and overgrown. Compelled by beauty, he left his friends and approached the building. As he pushed open the door, he smelled a strong stench and saw in the smoky interior a little pond in the dirt floor in which ducks swam. Beyond it a very old woman wrapped in a cloak and muttering to herself hunched before a peat fire, over which a pot was suspended. 'Here', he thought, 'is the Bronze Age or Iron Age virtually unchanged: hanging "cauldron", old hag muttering "spells" by an open fire, the litter of human habitation, apart from the cow-herd, who looked like the daughter of the High King of all Eire.' But the young peasant princess was nowhere to be seen.[13] It was as if he had walked into a tale about a *caillêch*, an Irish hag who had temporarily transformed herself into a young beauty.

This experience is in some respects a counterpart to his sight of the Mass north of Ypres the previous year. He would frequently recall both, and they therefore seem psychologically revelatory, like recurrent dreams. In both episodes he is alone approaching a building. In the first, he wanders a cold wasteland and is drawn by desire for warmth; in the second he walks in the lush green countryside and is drawn by feminine beauty. In the first, desire for warmth brings him to a numinous religious sight hidden indoors. In the second, feminine beauty vanishes in stench, smoke, and muttering old age. As a young boy, he had already experienced something like a paradigm for this second incident in the gradual disappearing of the benign gentleness

75. Nadolig Llawen, 1918

NADOLIG LLAWEN

of his maternal grandmother into senility. For him, the meaning of these oft-narrated wartime incidents may involve the contrasting implications for him of religion and sex. The first involved surprising fulfilment and inward liberation; the second threatened disappointment.

In addition to the beauty of the countryside and of its young women, he experienced as never before the 'exceptional beauty & great virility' of the English language as spoken by the Irish, which he would subsequently be able convincingly to imitate and would recognise and appreciate 'monumentally' in the writing of James Joyce, especially *Finnegans Wake*.[14]

He also gained extensive experience of a Celtic temperament different from that of the Welsh. The Irish were light-hearted and optimistic. Their ability to find something funny in the least likely circumstances amazed him. On one occasion at a train station, he watched an Irishman roar with laughter after just missing the last train home for 24 hours.[15]

Jones was waiting to be posted back to his unit in France, but on

11 November, during the manoeuvres near Cork in which he saw the beautiful young woman, the Armistice was declared.

He had survived the war – his only accomplishment that would surprise those who later came to know him. He marched in triumph with his battalion down Limerick's O'Connor Street. On 22 November his marksmanship was tested for the last time, and, perhaps because the Armistice improved his morale, he was rated a second-class shot. Also on the 22nd, he bought David Hume's *The History of England* (1828).

He drew a picture for a Christmas card, over the title HAPPY CHRISTMAS in Welsh, depicting an infantryman holding the hands of a female resembling, again, Elsie Hancock, here in traditional Welsh dress (fig. 75). He sent it to his father to have it reproduced. It is headed 'New Barracks, Limerick' and includes the words

> Christmas comes round, and a fifth New Year,
>   But what a different story:
> Let's drink a toast to the Fusilier,
>   Blighty, Home and Glory,

and is signed 'W DAVID JONES 1918'.

In his excitement he made, also this year, a second Christmas card entitled SIC SEMPER TYRANNIS (fig. 76), depicting an angelic victor holding a sword by the blade, delivering a still-distraught damsel from a vanquished German soldier. Inside the card he writes:

The Festival of Yule, 1918
Let those who are my friends accept this message as a token of my lasting regard for them. Never has the Season of the Nativity meant quite so much to each one of us as in the present year. To those among you who mourn the fallen, may I offer my most sincere sympathy? They surely did not die vainly. Through their splendid sacrifice the brutish gods of the Teuton lie despoiled and broken. Justice and meek-eyed Compassion

stand unshrouded before the eyes of the distressed people. Let us, then, with cheerfulness of heart, step into the sunlight of a New Day, ever keeping in remembrance the sacred dead who preserved for us so great an heritage.

He was ordered to go to Wimbledon to be 'disembodied', meaning to be transferred to Reserve, from which he could be called up if the truce failed. Just before leaving Ireland, he entered a latrine, leaning his rifle against the wall outside, and emerged to find it gone, stolen for use by rebels. He was frantic. To lose your rifle is among the worst of military crimes. He had no choice but to leave Ireland without it and decided to postpone confessing the loss until the last possible moment. On 18 December, at Wimbledon, with mounting anxiety, he walked up to the desk where he was supposed to turn in his rifle and receive his certificate of disembodiment. Nearby, he noticed a stack of recently turned-in rifles and quickly took one and handed it over as his own. After receiving his certificate and his campaign medal, the

76. Sic Semper Tyrannis, *1918*

1914–15 Star, he walked away, convinced that someone would check the serial number and discover his ruse. Back in Brockley in his parents' house, he waited anxiously for the military police, convinced that sooner or later they would come for him. Only gradually, over several months, did his anxiety decrease.[16]

Unlike most of his generation but with characteristic, impressive perspective, he would not regard the war as an important historic watershed. It was not comparable, he thought, to events of the sixteenth and seventeenth centuries, to the Napoleonic Wars, or to the Industrial Revolution, of which it was such a terrible manifestation. It would be, however, the single most important event in his life, occupying the last four of his most formative years and indelibly staining the litmus of his identity. Decades afterwards, if a door slammed, a car backfired, or someone dropped a walking-stick, the noise startled him back to the trenches. In distant thunder, he heard artillery. An Ancient Mariner of the western front, he frequently repeated war stories. In his final years he said about the war, 'the memory of it is like a disease . . . I still think about it more than anything else'.[17]

NOTES TO CHAPTER 8

1 DJ MS frag. n.d.; letter draft, frag. n.d.; to Harman Grisewood, 12 December 1966.
2 To Harman Grisewood, 1 February 1971.
3 To René Hague, 8 June 1966.
4 To Harman Grisewood, 12 December 1966; DJ to Blissett, p. 128; to Jim Ede, 23 August 1946. Jones is identifiable in the photograph only because he writes on the back, 'Eileen G with Salkeld & myself in E's white tamoshanter [sic].' Behind him in the photograph stands a third soldier, also obscured.
5 To Harman Grisewood, 12 December 1966.
6 DJ to Blissett, p. 24; Hague, *David Jones*, p. 51; René Hague interviewed by Peter Orr, 15 February 1977; John Montague, interviewed 9 September 1989; René Hague to Catherine Carter, 3 July 1980. Blissett remembers DJ saying that a colonel altered the charge (p. 32), but only the officer who put Jones on charge could have altered it.
7 DJ in 1970 to John Montague, interviewed 9 September 1989; DJ in conversation with Tony Stoneburner, written record 26 May 1969.
8 DJ in conversation with Tony Stoneburner, written record 26 May 1969.
9 DJ interviewed by Jon Silkin, 1971; DJ in conversation with Tony Stoneburner, written record 26 May 1969.

10 Charlie Bartlett (interviewed 11 June 1992) remembers Limerick as it was and at the age of four saw the RWF on church parade with their goat. DJ in conversation with author, 31 August 1972; John Montague, 'From *The Great Bell*', *David Jones: Man and Poet*, p. 83; DJ in conversation with Tony Stoneburner, written record 26 May 1969.

11 To Dorothea Travis, 26 December 1948.

12 DJ in conversation with Tony Stoneburner, written record, 26 May 1969; to Denis Tegetmeier, 26 December 1948.

13 To Denis Tegetmeier, 26 December 1948; DJ to Blissett, p. 129; John Montague, interviewed 9 September 1989; to René Hague, January 1955; to Harman Grisewood, 12 December 1966; *RQ* 101.

14 To Vernon Watkins, 5 April 1962.

15 DJ in conversation with author, 31 August 1972.

16 To Saunders Lewis, April 1971; DJ to Blissett, p. 129; Stanley Honeyman, interviewed June 1986.

17 DJ MS frag. n.d.; 'Sign of the bear, David Jones talks to Nesta Roberts'; Jim Ede, interviewed June 1985; *Manchester Guardian*, 11 February 1972.

CHAPTER 9

LOOSE ENDS

Leslie Poulter

Early in 1919 Jones renewed his friendship with Leslie Poulter. They were both dissatisfied with civilian life and felt that the end of the war had brought merely an extended leave. After so much anticipation, peace seemed inferior to conditions preceding the war and hardly worth the enormous cost. He and Poulter now distrusted politicians, despised political rhetoric, and lived in a public world to which they felt they could never belong. London seemed an alien place, except for the screaming of tram cars, which sounded exactly like in-coming shells.[1]

They longed for lost fellowship and the reality of combat, discussed the furious fighting that had broken out in Russia between the White and Red Armies, and decided to join the fight against Bolshevism. The press had reported that the Bolsheviks had executed thousands of former officers for violating a law against possessing firearms, had attacked the British embassy, killing four people, one a British subject, and were closing churches and persecuting Christians. He and Poulter decided to join the British Archangel Expedition, and Jones announced this to his parents. His father shared his political antipathy to Bolshevism but argued against his going again to war and managed finally to persuade him. Poulter went alone, fighting as a member of the North Russian Expeditionary Force until the end of 1920.[2]

When he returned, fluent in Russian, Jones and he again resumed their friendship. Poulter worked with a watch company until marrying, in 1924, an adamant Prince-Edward-Island Protestant named Amy Star – Jones attending the wedding. Poulter then worked for the railroad and played rugby for the London Welsh. He and his wife then lived for some years in West Africa before setting up house in Lewisham near Brockley.

Like so many ex-servicemen, Poulter was a psychological casualty of war. He was always now slightly depressed, lacked ambition, and failed to attain a position corresponding to his intelligence, education, and abilities. His income was and would remain minimal.

Jones and he met in pubs, where they may sometimes have been joined by their fellow ex-Fusilier, Harry Cook, with whom Jones remained in touch until Cook became involved in embezzlement and committed suicide. Jones also visited Poulter at his house in Lewisham, but Amy Poulter was unfriendly. Conventional, dominant, and stubborn, she considered artists disreputable, disliked Catholics, and thought Jones a freeloader. In 1934, the Poulters moved to 10 Vanbrugh Park, Blackheath, and Jones once visited them there, talking with Leslie late into the night and staying over. (His parents' house was nearby in Brockley, but he was living mostly now in Chelsea at the house of his friends the Burns brothers – Tom, an editor, and Charles, a psychiatrist.) In the morning he departed the Poulter house without emptying the chamber-pot under his bed – an unforgivable offence to Amy, who forbade further visits to the house. Jones and Leslie continued seeing one another in pubs, but less frequently. Jones gave him a copy of *In Parenthesis* and had the feeling that he disliked the use in it of coarse army language.

With the outbreak of Second World War in 1939, Poulter cheered up and worked for the Intelligence Service, M.I.6. As a spy, he was sent into Dakar in French West Africa to report on prospects for the success of 'Menace', Churchill's planned attack. He informed the War Office that the plan was hopeless, but his report was not passed on to the Joint Chiefs, and Churchill went ahead with the assault, which was disastrous. Resented for having been right, Poulter was marginalised, and his career in military intelligence stagnated, ending in 1943. He worked for a fireworks company, then for the railway as a clerk. In 1952 he died of cancer or kidney failure (he suffered from both), having remained all his life a devout Catholic, to the perpetual chagrin of his wife, who wrote to Jones informing him of his death.[3]

Harold Weaver Hawkins and Frank Medworth

In the Queen's Westminster Rifles, Harold Hawkins had been a regimental signaller for a year and nine months before being assigned to a sacrificial attack at Gommecourt on 1 July 1916, in which most in his unit were killed. He was shot through the right calf, the right arm, the chest, and the right shoulder-blade, and his right armpit was torn open by shrapnel. Left for dead, he spent two days dragging himself back to the British line. After 32 surgical operations, he was able to use his right hand but not his right arm and his left arm but not the fingers of that hand. So he now painted by using his left forearm to support his right hand, which could hold a brush. A lifelong disability pension made him financially independent.[4]

Frank Medworth had fought in the East Surrey Regiment at First Ypres and at the Somme, where he had lost part of the right side of the back of his skull so that his brain now lay directly beneath the skin in an opening in the skull the size of an egg. Sometimes, for fun, he closed his mouth and nose and blew to make the skin over the hole bulge. To protect his brain, he wore a cloth-covered metal plate resembling an oversize yarmulke. While recovering from his head-wound, he had himself declared fit for service, joined the King's African Rifles, and fought in Kenya. During years in sergeants' messes, he deliberately exaggerated his native Cockney accent, which, now, after the war, he tried hard to lose, affecting an upper-class accent and uttering mottoes and clichés in Latin and Greek.[5]

Jones, Medworth, and Hawkins resumed their triple friendship, a relationship now deepened by shared military experience. Together, in the autumn of 1919, they re-enrolled at the Camberwell School of Arts and Crafts, applying for and receiving government training grants to study 'Commercial Design and Illustration' for two years. For each year, the award paid £7 for tuition fees and a subsistence

77. The Three Musketeers: from left to right, Medworth, Hawkins and Jones, March 1919

allowance of £121. Jones was glad to be no longer financially depend-ent on his parents, though in the early post-war years he continued living with them. He, Hawkins and Medworth began calling them-selves 'The Three Musketeers', intending it as a sort of corporate name. They sought to establish themselves as a 'group' in hopes of attracting attention, selling pictures, and finding commercial work. They launched their business by going together, each with a portfolio, to the galleries in Bond Street. The work they showed elicited little comment, and, according to Medworth, Jones would mutter to the dealers about the pictures, 'They're not very good, are they? They're pretty rotten.' (In 1960, to Hawkins's younger brother Ernest, Jones denied ever having made such remarks.) He was no self-promoter, but neither were the other two. They disliked dealers and were unwilling to ingratiate themselves to further their careers. In March 1919, they donned their uniforms to have their photographs taken at Camber-well Art School (fig. 77).[6]

About art, they were, Jones would remember, 'pretty single-minded'. They attended a Kensington open life-class, which they had frequented before the war and which now seemed to him a relic of the Whistlerian past. He recognised many of those attending from before the war, some having continued for years 'laboriously doing excruci-atingly bad drawings – but awfully nice chaps – very courteous'. They argued a lot about art – some, Medworth foremost among them, convinced they would be great artists. All were poor, and Jones later remembered, 'we thought we were the saddest of men' although 'it was jolly nice'. In the summer of 1919, he and Hawkins, sometimes with Medworth, went on sketching trips into the countryside of Kent and Surrey.[7]

With the exception of one teacher, Camberwell School of Arts and Crafts was no longer, as it had been before the war, an interesting place. The exception was a 50-year-old painter and art critic named Walter Bayes. Early in the winter term of 1920, Bayes resigned from Camberwell to replace his mentor Walter Sickert as headmaster at Westminster School of Art. He urged The Three Musketeers to move with him. 'Under his spell', as Hawkins's younger brother remembered, they notified the school of their intention to leave. On 27 February 1920, the Advisory Sub-Committee at Camberwell registered a protest over losing 'the oldest and most advanced pupils of the school', but Jones and his friends had their government grants transferred and departed in March for the Westminster School of Art, in the Westminster Technical Institute at 77 Vincent Square.[8]

It was the smallest, least prestigious, least funded of the central London art schools. Jones attended classes taught by Bayes, Randolph Schwabe and Bernard Meninsky, and listened to weekly lectures by Walter Sickert, who remained the *genius loci* of the school. Encouraged by Jones's friend and former teacher A. S. Hartrick, Jones and his friends rejected the techniques Sickert prescribed, but they were, as he put it, 'school of Sickert', imitating his manner of drawing and painting – even though, they realised, current fashion was turning against Sickert's Impressionist style. Jones liked Sickert as a person and considered him second only to Turner among British painters, but the only technical teaching of Sickert that remained important to him concerned the changing values of colour tones depending on the colours with which they are juxtaposed.[9]

Hawkins bought a house at 6 Margravine Gardens in Barons Court with the help of his parents and his disability pension. He used it as a residence and studio, sharing it with other artists and two of his brothers. For a while Medworth was a tenant. Jones visited and worked in the studio. Here he got to know Hawkins's sixteen-year-old brother Ernest, who assumed at the time, as did his brother and Medworth, that Jones was suffering from shell-shock. Ernest was then interested in Catholicism and spent hours discussing religion with his brother, Medworth and Jones. Harold Hawkins, now going by his middle name, Weaver, was vehemently anti-clerical and opposed to all religious observance. Among the artists who visited the studio were the sculptor L. Cubit Bevis, a wounded ex-serviceman and a student at Westminster; the lithographer A. R. Laird; and the stained-glass designer James Hogan, the director of the Whitefriars Glassworks and designer of the

78. David Jones in Hawkins's studio, early 1920s

windows for Liverpool Cathedral and St Patrick's Cathedral in New York. 'Discussions on all subjects . . . were', Weaver Hawkins would remember, 'continuous, entertaining, informative, enlightening'. At Hawkins's urging, Jones and Medworth began seeing plays.[10]

Jones would go to Hawkins's studio by himself or with Medworth. There Hawkins's brother Wilfred photographed Jones sitting in a wicker chair, his hair combed back, in the direction he characteristically pushed it as he worked or talked (fig. 78). His suit was a ginger-coloured tweed made of cloth loom-woven for him by Eric Gill's daughter Petra – Jones having become involved in Gill's commune of Catholic craftsmen at Ditchling. It was, Ernest Hawkins remembered 60 years later, the hairiest tweed he ever saw.[11]

Jones and Weaver Hawkins lost touch with each other after Hawkins married in 1923 and began living in various places around the Mediterranean before moving to Australia in 1935. Hawkins's marriage lasted, producing three children, and, despite his war wounds, he had a successful career. He died in 1977.

Medworth taught at Westminster School of Art. He and Jones continued for years meeting for a weekly 'pub crawl'. Medworth was keeping company with a Westminster student named Muriel (Mog) Anderson. The two of them went on holiday to Spain to visit Weaver Hawkins and were married in Barcelona by the British consul. When they returned, Mog was pregnant and Medworth, who had learned that the marriage was not legal since they had not been long enough in Spain before the wedding, had cold feet. He sought the advice of Jones, who told him, 'There's no question about it. You'll have to marry the girl.' The official ceremony took place on 5 July 1929 at the Chelsea Registry Office, with Jones and Eric Gill as witnesses. By then, the bride was over eight months pregnant, a sight that greatly amused Gill.[12]

Jones and Medworth continued meeting for pints and conversation. Medworth was probably an important sounding-board for military matters during the composition of *In Parenthesis* – until January 1934, when he left London to become principal at the City of Hull College of Arts and Crafts. He, his wife and their daughter subsequently emigrated to Australia, where he became principal of Sydney Art School and resumed his friendship with Hawkins. In 1947, despite parliamentary protests over his association with socialists, he was chosen as Australian delegate to a UNESCO conference in Mexico City. At the conference, on 11 November, he gave a nonsensical speech, attributed by listeners to drunkenness but actually caused by diminished air pressure in the high altitude forcing his brain to expand into the hole in his skull. After the speech he went back to his hotel, got into the bathtub, slashed his wrists, and died – a delayed casualty of the Battle of the Somme. Jones would always regard him as an 'astounding man'.[13]

A. S. Hartrick

Shortly after returning home in December 1918, Jones fell ill with flu for the first time in four years. His first excursion to London was on 3 January 1919, with his certificate of disembodiment to apply for unemployment benefits and to visit Hartrick. His former teacher was no longer at Camberwell but at the Central School of Art. Having been considered advanced by the art-world before the war, he was now regarded as passé. Over subsequent years, Hartrick went to exhibitions of Jones's visual art, and Jones sometimes visited him at his home for a meal. In 1948, the man who had taught him to draw with the point informed him of a new technological wonder: a pen that 'makes a line always of one thickness' – the Bic ballpoint pen, which Jones became enamoured of (largely because such pens came with different coloured inks) and used to write with for the rest of his life. In 1950, not having seen him in almost two years and intending to visit soon, Jones read in the paper of Hartrick's death on 1 February. He wrote a letter to *The Times* (unpublished) in which he says that Hartrick's work deserves more appreciation, that he was 'individual, sensitive, & disinterested', that his best work is, compared to that of Charles Keene, 'more tentative, with more signs of struggle, less accomplished, more surpriseful, with more sense of design & understanding of form'. He recalls that Hartrick had been innately humble, that having been considered 'advanced' in his youth and, since then, 'out-moded' had mattered little to him. For Hartrick the important thing had been to 'do the work'. More than anyone else Jones had known, he had been a model of what an artist should be as a person.[14]

David Jones

At Ditchling in Sussex, with Gill's commune of craftsmen, Jones learned to engrave in wood and was in the vanguard of the revival of the art form in England. He produced remarkable wood engravings, including those in *The Chester Play of the Deluge* (1927), which is a masterpiece of book illustration. He taught himself to engrave in copper, and, in that medium, illustrated *The Rime of the Ancient Mariner* (1929), another masterpiece.* In 1924 he became engaged to Petra Gill but, unable to imagine supporting a family as an artist, dragged his heels and became inattentive. She broke the engagement in 1927 to marry a mutual friend. Jones painted increasingly in watercolours and, in 1926, burned most of his early artwork. By 1926, he was a friend of Jim Ede, the Tate curator who would make Henri Gaudier-Brzeska famous. Ede admired Jones's work and successfully urged Ben Nicholson to recruit Jones into the Seven and Five Society, which was the most exciting group of artists then exhibiting in London. It included Ben and Winifred Nicholson and Christopher Wood and would soon include Frances Hodgkins, Barbara Hepworth and Henry Moore. Jones's work sold more than that of any other member of the group.

In 1929 he became involved with a gathering of Catholic intellectuals influenced by the French neo-Thomist philosopher Jacques Maritain, which met at the changing Chelsea addresses of the Tom and

---

* Jones's illustrations for *The Deluge* are reproduced and interpreted in my *Reading David Jones* (Cardiff: University of Wales, 2008), pp. 9–19; those for Coleridge's poem are reproduced and interpreted in my edition of *The Rime of the Ancient Mariner* (London: Enitharmon Press, 2005), pp. 46-106. In each of these I indicate the importance of Jones's wedding of temporal-literary form and spatial-visual form as precedents for the unifying structures of his subsequent long poems.

Charles Burns until the start of the Second World War. Members of the group included the historian Christopher Dawson, with whom Jones became friends, and Jones's closest friends the Burns brothers, Harman Grisewood and René Hague. Not in the group but one of the most important people in his life throughout the 1930s was a brilliant young woman named Prudence Pelham. She was the muse of *In Parenthesis* and the unnamed friend whom he thanks 'very especially' in its preface (*IP* xv).

He read most of the books on the Great War by ex-servicemen, including, in 1929, Erich Maria Remarque's *All Quiet on the Western Front*, translated by Jones's friend Arthur Wheen. Putting it down after finishing it, he said in the hearing of Tom Burns, 'Bugger it, I can do better than that. I'm going to write a book.'[15] In 1928 he had already begun experimenting with drawing-and-writing based on his war experience. Now he began writing his epic of the Great War in earnest, knowing from the start that its title would be *In Parenthesis*. In 1932, the completion of its first continuous draft brought on a devastating nervous breakdown and severe depression, which delayed publication until 1937.

In Parenthesis is written with a vividness that makes immediately real the physicality of war, but it is also highly allusive. In 1975 Paul Fussell in his influential book *The Great War and Modern Memory* would misread it as glorifying the war by alluding to romances – but Jones had by then come a long way from the idealistic drawings he had published during the war. The principal effect of the allusions in *In Parenthesis* is symbolically to align the Battle of the Somme with the defeat of Roland at Roncesvalles and Celtic historical and legendary catastrophes that are symbolically subsumed by the Battle of Camlan, which, in the romance tradition, brought to an end Arthur's Celtic Britain. Allusions to romance express with archetypal force the horror of modern war and the powerful poignancy of the deaths of infantrymen. At the centre of the book, Dai Greatcoat, the archetypal soldier, says, 'You ought to ask: Why, . . . what's the meaning of this' (*IP* 84). It is a question about war but also about life. A clue to an answer lies in Malory's Beaumains (alluded to on *IP* 119), whose employment as a kitchen-boy disguises his true character. The implication is of the usually unseen virtues (courage, patience, kindness, affection), and the significance of this implication is that the meaning of war and of life in general resides in, or is indicated by, human goodness. In his poem, Jones reconfigures the tradition of war and reveals new meaning in previous literary works – revealing, for example, the violence inherent in *Through the Looking-Glass* and showing *Henry V* to be an incipient problem play with a strong anti-war theme.

In 1938 *In Parenthesis* won the Hawthorndon Prize, then the only important British literary award, and was praised at length by W. B. Yeats speaking personally to Jones (at the Chichester estate near Brighton, in the company of Prudence Pelham and Edward Hodgkin). T. S. Eliot considered it a 'deeply' moving 'work of genius'.[16] W. H. Auden declared it 'a masterpiece' and, in 1954, 'the greatest book about the First World War'.[17] In 1980, Graham Greene judged it 'among the great poems of the century'.[18] *In Parenthesis* is the greatest work of literature on the Great War and arguably the greatest work on war in English. In the years immediately after publication, however, few involved in the Second World War were interested in reading about the prior war. As a consequence and because its publisher, Faber and Faber, neglected to list or describe it as a poem (until 1988) or to list Jones among the Faber poets, *In Parenthesis* was slow to be recognised as a long poem and, consequently, was lost for decades to critical or academic assessment and appreciation. The first adequate critical assessment – and the one Jones most liked – was John H. Johnston's 'The Heroic Vision: David Jones' in his *English Poetry of the First World War* (1964), pp. 284–340. It remains one of the best essays on the poem.

Depression continued to afflict Jones, allowing him to paint only occasionally. Immediately after hearing his friend Douglas Cleverdon's radio broadcast of *In Parenthesis* in 1947, he suffered a second crushing breakdown. He received psychological treatment from a gifted therapist named Bill Stevenson, who explained to him that he had been more frightened during the war than he realised and urged him to return to visual art and continue writing.

With Stevenson's psychological help, he resumed painting, so that an exhibition of new paintings could take place in 1948, and wrote *The Anathemata* (1952), his second epic-length poem, which is a symbolic-dramatic anatomy of western culture. W. H. Auden regarded it as 'one of the most important poems of our time' and called it, in 1977, 'probably the finest long poem in English' of the twentieth century.[19] For various reasons, including its unique, unifying structure, *The Anathemata* may well be the greatest modern long poem and the most important single work of British Modernism. Academic critical response was delayed by the failure of Faber and Faber to list or describe it as poetry until 1970.* But on the basis of this work and its predecessor, in 1962 Igor Stravinsky considered Jones 'perhaps the greatest living writer in English'[20] and in 1964, Herbert Read called him 'one of the greatest writers of our time'.[21]

Jones continued to paint, concentrating in the 1950s on marvellous still lifes of flowers in glass chalices and in the 1960s on large multicoloured inscriptions. Many of these and two of his final mythic figure paintings (*Trystan ac Esyllt*, 1963, and *Annunciation in a Welsh Hill Setting*, 1963) are masterpieces. Cheated repeatedly and in various ways since 1948 by the owner of the Redfern Gallery, Rex Nan Kivell, he refused to exhibit his work in galleries, apart from the Tate Gallery retrospective of his work in 1954–5.

After 1941 he lived and worked in a single rented room, moving from central London in 1948 to Harrow. There he became increasingly agoraphobic, staying in his room, which he called his 'dugout'. Deeply intelligent in conversation and warmly affectionate, he had many friends, among them Kenneth Clark and T. S. Eliot, and he received

---

*The first substantial interpretation of the work is Neil Corcoran, *Song of Deeds: a Study of* The Anathemata *of David Jones* (Cardiff: University of Wales, 1982); the most thorough interpretation is my *The Shape of Meaning in the Poetry of David Jones* (Toronto: University of Toronto, 1988), pp. 152–257. My *Reading David Jones* contains the clearest summary of the poem, pp. 116–175.

a steady stream of visitors, including people who considered him a great writer, such as W. H. Auden, Louis Zukofsky and Igor Stravinsky.

On 15 July 1964 Jones met and had a long talk with Siegfried Sassoon, with whom he spoke about the Welch Fusiliers at Mametz and Limerick. Sassoon said that however much he tried he could not get the First World War out of his system and that this was true also for Edmund Blunden. Jones said it was true also for him.[22]

In 1970 he suffered minor strokes and a bad fall and went into a nursing home. In 1974, he published *The Sleeping Lord*, a collection of mid-length poems, which the American poet W. S. Merwin regards as among 'his greatest splendours'.[23] They are his most accessible poems and include 'The Hunt', and 'The Tutelar of the Place', which are, because so lyrically musical, probably the first poems anyone new to his work should read. In 1974 he was made a Companion of Honour, and, on 28 October 1974, he died in bed.

Elsie Hancock

Jones never forgot Elsie. After resuming civilian life in 1918, he and she continued writing to each other. In the spring or summer of 1919, he visited her, staying a few days at her parents' house in Shipston-on-Stour. They went together to Stratford to see a Shakespearean comedy, which he disliked (as he did most of Shakespeare's comedies), and, on their final day together, visited Banbury Cross. The reunion was not what he had hoped. Having become engaged, to Thomas Montague Bullock, before meeting Jones, she was unwilling to break her engagement. She and Jones parted and never met again. She married and lived, childless, into old age. At the end of his life Jones confided that his feelings for her had never been 'wholly eradicated' but resembled prehistoric earthworks that 'aerial photography reveals as though they were digged yesterday'.[24]

NOTES TO CHAPTER 9

1 Anne Beresford, 'A Friendship with David Jones – a personal account', typescript, n.d.

2 David Poulter to author, 9 February 1990; DJ to Blissett, p. 133.

3 David Poulter, interviewed 11 June 1990; DJ to Arthur Pritchard-Williams, 15 December 1954.

4 *The South London Press*, 15 March 1918; Chanin and Miller, pp. 33, 36.

5 Ernest Hawkins to author, 29 April 1988; Diana Macartney-Filgate to author, 18 April 1991; Ernest Hawkins, interviewed 15 June 1988.

6 Announcement of Award, Reg. No O, 40366/19; DJ, 'Autobiographical details given to Douglas Cleverdon, 3 July 1970'; Stella Wright and Kathleen Lockitt, interviewed 21 June 1989; Valentine Kilbride in conversation with Tony Stoneburner, written record 3 June 1969: Medworth in the 1920s remembered by Ernest Hawkins, interviewed 1 August 1987.

7 To Harman Grisewood, 24 August 1956; Ernest Hawkins, interviewed 1 August 1987.

8 Ernest Hawkins, interviewed 1 August 1987, 15 June 1988.

9 To Tony Stoneburner, 24–5 October 1969; *LF* 15.

10 Ernest Hawkins, interviewed 25 August 1989, 1 August 1987; Chanin and Miller, p. 42.

11 Ernest Hawkins, interviewed 1 September 1987, 15 June 1988; Petra Tegetmeier, interviewed 3 October 1987.

12 Ernest Hawkins, interviewed 15 June 1988; Diana McCartney-Filgate to Elizabeth Skelton, 18 April 1980; to Eric Gill, 14 June 1936.

13 Ernest Hawkins, interviewed 15 June 1988; Diana McCartney-Filgate to Elizabeth Skelton, 18 April 1980; to Eric Gill, 14 June 1936; to Francis Wall, 27 June 1944; Ernest Hawkins, interviewed 1 August 1987; Elizabeth Skelton, interviewed 12 June 1990; entries in the Medworth family bible.

14 A. S. Hartrick to DJ, 2 March 1948; to René Hague, 9 September 1974; 'Note to *The Times*', Christmas 1963; 'Note on MS', draft n.d. [1951]; letter draft to *The Times*. n.d.; to Helen Sutherland, 9 September 1951; to Harman Grisewood, 14 February 1950; Hartrick to DJ, 2 March 1948; to Patrick Kelly, unposted frag., 22 December 1954.

15 Tom Burns saw him put down the book and heard him say these words. Burns, interviewed 14 June 1989.

16 Eliot, 'A Note of Introduction' (1961), *IP* vii.

17 'The Geste says this and the man who was on the field', *Mid-Century Review* 39 (March 1962), pp. 12, 13.

18 *Ways of Escape* (Toronto: Lester & Orpen Dennys, 1980), p. 28.

19 *A Certain World* (New York: Viking, 1970), p. 373.

20 Robert Craft, *Retrospectives and Conclusions* (New York: Knopf, 1969), pp. 227–8.

21 To John H. Johnston, 25 April 1964.

22 To Harman Grisewood, 17 July 1964.

23 Merwin, letter to author, 7 April 2009.

24 DJ interviewed by Peter Orr, early 1970s; to Janet Stone, 7–8 July 1972.

BIBLIOGRAPHY

Auden, W. H. *A Certain World* (New York: Viking, 1970).
    'The Geste says this and the man who was on the field', *Mid-Century Review* 39 (March 1962), 12–13.
Blamires, David. 'The Medieval Inspiration of David Jones', *David Jones: Eight Essays*, ed. Roland Mathias (Llandysul: Gomer Press, 1976), 73–7.
Blissett, William. *The Long Conversation: a memoir of David Jones* (Oxford: Oxford University Press, 1981).
Chanin, Eileen and Steven Miller. *The Art and Life of Weaver Hawkins* (Roseville, New South Wales: Craftsman House, 1995).
Chasseaud, Peter. *Topography of Armageddon, a British Trench Map Atlas of the Western Front 1914–1918* (Lewes: Mapbooks, 1991).
    'David Jones and the Survey', *David Jones, Artist and Poet*, ed. Paul Hills (Aldershot: Scolar Press: 1997), 18–30.
Cleverdon, Douglas and David Jones. *Word and Image* (London: National Book League, 1972).
Craft, Robert. *Retrospectives and Conclusions* (New York, Knopf, 1969).
Dilworth, Thomas. 'A Try Out: David Jones's "A French Vision"', *London Magazine* 33 (April–May 1993), 73–9.
    Reading David Jones (Cardiff: University of Wales Press, 2008).
Eliot, T. S. 'A Note of Introduction', *In Parenthesis* (London: Faber & Faber, 1961), vii–viii.
Ellis, John. *Eye-Deep in Hell: Trench Warfare in World War I* (Baltimore: Johns Hopkins University, 1976).
Greene, Graham. *Ways of Escape* (Toronto: Lester & Orpen Dennys, 1980).
Griffith, Llywelyn Wyn. *Up to Mametz* (London: Faber & Faber, 1931).
Fussell, Paul. *The Great War and Modern Memory* (Oxford: Oxford University Press, 2000).
Hague, René. *David Jones* (Cardiff: University of Wales Press, 1975).

Hartrick, A. S. *A Painter's Pilgrimage Through Fifty Years* (Cambridge: Cambridge University Press, 1939).

    Drawing (London: Pitman, 1921).

Heaney, Seamus. 'Now and in England', *Spectator* (4 May 1974), 547.

Hughes, Colin. *David Jones: The Man Who Was on the Field*: In Parenthesis *as Straight Reporting* (Manchester: David Jones Society, 1979).

Ironside, Robin. *David Jones* (Harmondsworth, Middlesex: Penguin, 1949).

Johnston, John H. *English Poetry of the First World War* (Princeton: Princeton University Press, 1964).

Jones, David. *The Anathemata* (London: Faber and Faber, 1972).

    The Chester Play of the Deluge, illustrated by David Jones (Bristol: Golden Cockerel, 1927).

    Dai Greatcoat, ed. René Hague (London: Faber & Faber, 1980).

    Epoch and Artist (London: Faber & Faber, 1959).

    'For the Front', *Tablet* (13 January 1940), 39–40.

    'Fragments of an Attempted Autobiographical Writing', *Agenda* 12:4–13:1 (Winter–Spring 1975), 96–108.

    A Fusilier at the Front, selected by Anthony Hyne (Bridgend: Seren, 1995)

    In Parenthesis (London: Faber & Faber 1978).

    Letter to *The Times*, 22 February 1961.

    The Rime of the Ancient Mariner by S. T. Coleridge, illustrated by David Jones, ed. Thomas Dilworth (London: Enitharmon Press, 2005).

    The Sleeping Lord (London: Faber & Faber, 1974).

    Wedding Poems, ed. Thomas Dilworth (London: Enitharmon Press, 2002).

Miles, Jonathan and Derek Shiel. *David Jones: The Maker Unmade* (Bridgend: Seren, 1995).

Montague, John. 'From *The Great Bell*', *David Jones: Man and Poet*, ed. John Matthias (Orono, Maine: National Poetry Foundation, 1989), 81–4.

Munby, Lt.-Col. J. E., ed. *A History of the 38th (Welsh) Division by the G.S.O.'s I of the Division* (London: Hugh Rees, 1920).

Roberts, Nesta. 'Sign of the bear, David Jones talks to Nesta Roberts', *Manchester Guardian*, 17 February 1964, 7.

Rosenberg, Harold. 'Aesthetics of Crisis', *New Yorker*, 22 August 1964, 114–122.

INDEX

FRIENDS OF ENITHARMON

The following have generously become Patrons and Sponsors of the *Friends of Enitharmon* scheme, enabling this and other publications to come into being:

PATRONS

Duncan Forbes
Sean O'Connor
Masatsugu Ohtake
Myra Schneider

SPONSORS

Kathy & Jeff Allinson
Colin Beer
Natasha Curry
Vanessa Davis
Jack Herbert
Alison M. Houston
Sylvia Riley
Angela Sorkin
Janet Upward